WILL CHINA PROTECT INTELLECTUAL PROPERTY? NEW DEVELOPMENTS IN COUNTERFEITING, PIRACY, AND FORCED TECHNOLOGY TRANSFER

HEARING

BEFORE THE

CONGRESSIONAL-EXECUTIVE COMMISSION ON CHINA

ONE HUNDRED ELEVENTH CONGRESS

SECOND SESSION

SEPTEMBER 22, 2010

Printed for the use of the Congressional-Executive Commission on China

Available via the World Wide Web: http://www.cecc.gov

U.S. GOVERNMENT PRINTING OFFICE

62–289 PDF   WASHINGTON : 2012

For sale by the Superintendent of Documents, U.S. Government Printing Office
Internet: bookstore.gpo.gov   Phone: toll free (866) 512–1800; DC area (202) 512–1800
Fax: (202) 512–2104   Mail: Stop IDCC, Washington, DC 20402–0001

(II)

CONTENTS

WILL CHINA PROTECT INTELLECTUAL PROPERTY? NEW DEVELOPMENTS IN COUNTERFEITING, PIRACY, AND FORCED TECHNOLOGY TRANSFER

WEDNESDAY, SEPTEMBER 22, 2010

CONGRESSIONAL-EXECUTIVE
COMMISSION ON CHINA,
Washington, DC.

The hearing was convened, pursuant to notice, at 2:18 p.m., in room 628, Dirksen Senate Office Building, Senator Byron Dorgan, Chairman, presiding.

Also present: Representative Sander Levin, Cochairman; and Senator Dianne Feinstein.

OPENING STATEMENT OF HON. BYRON DORGAN, A U.S. SENATOR FROM NORTH DAKOTA, CHAIRMAN, CONGRESSIONAL-EXECUTIVE COMMISSION ON CHINA

Chairman DORGAN. I'm going to call the hearing to order.

This is a hearing of the Congressional-Executive Commission on China. I'm Senator Byron Dorgan, Chairman of the Commission. We will be joined momentarily by other members of the Commission.

The hearing today is on the subject of: "Will China Protect Intellectual Property? New Developments in Counterfeiting, Piracy, and Forced Technology Transfer."

This country has a relationship with China that is very important, and will become even more important going forward. That relationship, however, has a number of very vexing, difficult issues attached to it, one of which is the issue of international trade. We run a very large trade deficit with the country of China. It is a deficit that is the highest trade deficit in the world with the United States.

We also are very concerned, and have long been concerned, with China with respect to the safeguarding of intellectual property, and have been concerned about piracy and counterfeiting on intellectual property and other goods coming from the United States.

I noticed in last week's Wall Street Journal a story that in many ways summarizes much of what concerns us, and one of the reasons that we have called this hearing. This hearing occurs a long while after the Congress passed PNTR [Permanent Normal Trade Relations] with China, and many of us had high hopes that there would be very dramatic changes as China joined the World Trade Organization [WTO] and China would take steps as a full partner

(1)

in the international community of trade to protect intellectual property and to shut down piracy and counterfeiting.

But China, in many ways, while making some progress and some success in other areas, in many ways China, I believe, has turned a blind eye to the issue of piracy and counterfeiting and has engaged in managed trade with the sole purpose of running a very large trade surplus with our country, or we a deficit with them, in a way that I think has been fundamentally unfair.

But the Wall Street Journal story of September 16 says the following:

> China's government is considering plans that would force foreign automakers to hand over cutting-edge electric vehicle technology to Chinese companies in exchange for access to the nation's huge market, international auto executives say.
> China's Ministry of Industry and Information Technology is preparing a 10-year plan aimed at turning China into a world's leader in developing and producing battery-powered cars and hybrids, according to executives at four car companies who are familiar with the proposal.
> The draft suggests that the government could compel foreign automakers that want to produce electric vehicles in China to share critical technologies by requiring the companies to enter into joint ventures in which they are limited to a minority stake, executives say.

Then, finally, the plan is "tantamount to China strong-arming foreign automakers to give up battery, electric motor, and control technology in exchange for market access in China." This is just last week, but it goes on.

It is interesting to me, in our trade relationship with China, we have this very large trade deficit, somewhere in the neighborhood of $250 billion a year. When we have trade negotiations and opportunities to work with the Chinese on trade—which should always be mutually beneficial if two partners negotiate trade issues, you ought to end up with something that is considered to be mutually beneficial—somehow we end up not quite in that area.

Intellectual property—for example, movies—after negotiations, we're able to see 20 foreign movies into the Chinese marketplace. Twenty. Is it a wonder, then, that there is massive copying, illegal copying, of that intellectual property and then distributed and sold on the streets of China? Not to me, it's not. If our market is open to Chinese goods, why should the Chinese market not be wide open to our goods?

It is not that the Chinese are not able to control counterfeiting and piracy. We had an interesting lesson with respect to the Olympics. The Olympic logo belonged to the Chinese Government. It was their property. When people on the streets of China began to take that logo and put it on pencils, and pennants, and so on and use it for their own purposes, the Chinese Government very effectively shut it down because that belonged to them. Demonstrating that they can shut this down ought to suggest to us that if they see this happening to American intellectual property, they could shut it down as well, but they choose not to.

China, I think, has failed to comply with its commitments to protect intellectual property rights. It made that promise when it joined the WTO. I think that failure has a direct impact here in this country. The impact: Americans out of work, American jobs shift to China, misery from American manufacturing workers who used to have good jobs that paid well, with good benefits, that are now this morning putting on their clothes and going out and looking for a job. That's the impact of all of this.

It has a profound impact on our country when you run a trade deficit of this size that represents a trade deficit intended by the Chinese Government, because of the managed trade system they wage, and also a trade deficit based on the kind of difficulty that we have making sure that our intellectual property is not hijacked in a foreign country, as has been the case in China too often.

There have been some things that represent good news in China. The government has reformed some of its legal infrastructure. It's amended its copyright, patent, and trademark laws in order to be compliant with WTO rules. But the question is not too much that. The question is, how are these things enforced? Is there really an intent to enforce these areas as a part of the international community and international trade?

Since China joined the WTO in 2001, we've seen about 2.5 million jobs lost in the United States due to the U.S.-China trade deficit, that is, our deficit with China. Some of the great American brand names no longer are American; they have long since moved to China in search of cheap labor and so on. That's an issue that's related, but somewhat different than copyright and intellectual property infringement and counterfeiting.

But the Chinese Government has really systematically refused to effectively police the black markets that exist for counterfeit and pirated goods. We had a USTR, U.S. Trade Representative's, 2010 Special 301 Report and it says, "Widespread IPR infringement continues to affect products, brands, and technologies from a wide range of industries."

China accounts for 79 percent of IPR-infringing goods smuggled into the United States. When you walk down the street of a major city—you walk down the street and see all kinds of people selling wristwatches, and purses, and scarves, and so on, most of it counterfeit. Our USTR says 79 percent of the intellectual property-infringing goods smuggled into the United States comes from China. That's $7.6 billion in 2009, a $900 million increase over 2008.

I won't talk about the market barriers and other related issues. I would just say that the healthy relationship that we hoped for and expect in the future with China is a relationship that does not now exist in international trade, and that relationship, in my judgment, must change.

We must expect China, which has now joined the WTO, to abide by the rules, to aggressively enforce intellectual property rights, to shut down the issues dealing with counterfeiting and piracy, and to take effective action to demonstrate to us they are ready to become full partners in international trade in the way that we understand international trade should be conducted.

It is also the case—and I have written a book about this subject of international trade—that it is unsustainable for us to have a $200–250 billion-a-year trade deficit with a single country. That's not sustainable and is going to have to change as well.

But with all of that, let me just say that this Commission has been active in pursuing a wide range of subjects. I have, and so has my colleague, Representative Levin, who chaired this Commission previously, indicated where appropriate that certain progress has been made in some areas of China, but there are many other areas that have not yet begun to see the kind of changes that are necessary.

Much of what we have done with this Commission has focused on those who have been sent to the darkest prisons of the rural areas of China for basic acts of free speech, and the violation of their human rights concerns us, and will always concern us. We, at this point, maintain the largest repository of information on prisoners in Chinese jails who are human rights prisoners, and we're going to continue to work on that. Today we're talking about a different subject: "Will China Protect Intellectual Property? New Developments in Counterfeiting, Piracy, and Forced Technology Transfer."

I am joined by my colleagues, Representative Levin and Senator Feinstein. Representative Levin, would you wish to make an opening comment?

STATEMENT OF HON. SANDER LEVIN, A U.S. REPRESENTATIVE FROM THE STATE OF MICHIGAN, COCHAIRMAN, CONGRESSIONAL-EXECUTIVE COMMISSION ON CHINA

Representative LEVIN. Thank you. It's my privilege to join you, Mr. Chairman and Senator Feinstein, during this uniquely busy time here in the Congress. You have covered the subject so well, so let me just add a few thoughts.

Senator Dorgan, I think you were so right to point out the work of this Commission. It has done invaluable work in terms of human rights, including labor rights. Its charge from the very beginning also related to the rule of law, and that's the basic subject here today. It's really, this hearing, of utmost importance to our businesses and our workers, in part because they lose billions of dollars every year through the infringement of intellectual property rights in China.

The Chinese Government has failed to comply with its commitments to protect intellectual property rights that it made in joining the WTO, and unfortunately it continues to undermine protections for intellectual property contained in its own laws, and so by shining a spotlight on this, the Commission has an important role to play. You mentioned, Senator Dorgan, the Wall Street Journal article. I think as we read it, we said to ourselves, something has to give.

Indeed, China's industrial policies have had a common thread. They have a purpose and the effect of tilting the playing field to favor Chinese companies and against U.S. companies and workers, and those in other countries. As you said, this is not either a sound or a sustainable basis for the important mutually beneficial U.S.-China relationship, nor is it a viable foundation for the development of rule of law in China.

Indeed, there is a widening chasm between what we hear from the Chinese Government about IPR protection and what we know to be true. For example, we hear that the legal infrastructure supporting intellectual property rights has improved. We hear that courts are becoming more professionalized and skilled at handling complex issues.

We hear that Chinese rights holders are turning to Chinese courts to assert their rights more than in the past, and that there's been a measurable increase in the number of civil intellectual property cases in Chinese courts. We hear that foreign plaintiffs are winning intellectual property cases at increasing rates.

That's what we hear, but this, unfortunately, is what we know: the American Chamber of Commerce in China surveyed its members this year, and found 63 percent rated intellectual property enforcement in China as "ineffective." We know IPR infringement in China is more widespread than before. Counterfeit exports have increased. We know that the enforcement of IPR judgments is difficult in China and damages are still inadequate. The Chinese Government has often taken insufficient steps to address these difficulties.

So in sum, we know that the Chinese Government could be doing far more—far, far more—to protect intellectual property rights. We know, for example, in 2009—and I'll just cover these briefly—79 percent of intellectual property infringement product seizures at the U.S. border were of Chinese origin.

We know that China's State-Owned Assets Supervision and Administration Commission has the power to require state-owned enterprises to certify that all software they use is properly licensed, but that hasn't been required. We know that the production of counterfeit parts experienced a period of significant growth in China relating to auto parts and beyond, and we know that Chinese Government access barriers lead consumers to the black market.

And let me say this very clearly: Chinese Government censorship leads consumers to the black market, and that in turn incentivizes the violation of IPR rights. The Chinese Government often denies the link between human rights and the commercial rule of law, but there is a clear link and the Chinese Government itself helps to create this link. There can be no doubt that Chinese flagrant abuse of international rules undermines the rule of law.

There is no doubt that widespread intellectual property rights infringement in China continues to affect—and you mentioned this, Mr. Chairman—products, brands, and technologies from a wide range of industries, and imperils the health and safety of both American and Chinese consumers, and imposes billions of dollars of losses yearly on American business and workers.That is why change is necessary, both in the Chinese Government's behavior and in the action we take in response. So this is an important hearing for us, for the entire Congress, for the country, and I think for China and our relationships, so we look forward eagerly to the testimony before us.

Thank you.

Chairman DORGAN. Congressman Levin, thank you very much.

Senator Feinstein, would you like to make an opening statement?

STATEMENT OF HON. DIANNE FEINSTEIN, A U.S. SENATOR FROM CALIFORNIA; MEMBER, CONGRESSIONAL-EXECUTIVE COMMISSION ON CHINA

Senator FEINSTEIN. Just a few. I come at this a little differently, and I want to thank you both for your concern. I mean, I've been going to China now for over 30 years, and I remember what life was like there before 30 years. I think we have to remember that. China is a country 5,000 years old. Prior to normalization in 1979, begun by the Shanghai communication in 1972, China had been closed to the west for 150 years. It had been run by emperors that were arbitrary, arrogant.

The transition from a rule of man to a rule of law, I think, has moved rather substantially in this 30-year period. It isn't there yet. It isn't what we want to see, but I think it has to be understood that movement is made. I have found in certain areas—and I'll give you one, on the piracy issue—I met with the President of China in the 1990s at the request of the motion picture industry and others, and I was assured that all the pirate companies in Guangdong had been closed. Somebody came in and gave me a list of 32 companies who owned them, where they were located, what they did. I sent this to the USTR, who then sent it to China, and they were all closed.

Now, either this is wilful avoidance, or certain people in the government really didn't know. I'm not making a plea for the government. I think the government has to begin to understand what cyber-intrusion is doing, what intellectual property rights mean. I come from a State where intellectual property rights are extraordinarily important. I mean, this is innovation. This is movement and they must be protected, and there are laws to protect them, patent laws, copyright laws, all of this. In the Judiciary Committee, we have a patent bill that has just come out.

The problem is, there is inconsistent dialogue. There is virtually not the kind of communication that should go on on an ongoing basis between officials of our government and officials of the Chinese Government. Constant, monthly working away at this. I think because of this long history of China, because so much of it just being the rule of man, that to get this to a modern commercial code, modern patents, a modern criminal code, is really an effort.

I just wanted to say that because I think it's easy to make the judgment that China doesn't want to do any of this. I don't necessarily believe that's correct. I think we have to really press this issue home because it's extraordinarily important to the relationship.

Chairman DORGAN. Senator Feinstein, thank you very much for your perspective. You and I have been together in Beijing, and I know that you have a long association with the country of China and have had a lot to do with sister cities and various things. So, thank you for that perspective as well. We appreciate that.

Senator FEINSTEIN. You're welcome.

Chairman DORGAN. We have four witnesses today. The first, is Christian Murck. Christian Murck is the president of the American Chamber of Commerce in the People's Republic of China. I'm told that he traveled here from Beijing yesterday to, among other things, come to this hearing. We appreciate it very much. You get the longest distance award today. We appreciate your willingness to make that effort.

He was, in 2002, elected as president of the American Chamber in China. He is also the independent director of J.P. Morgan Chase Limited in China. From 2001 to March 2010, he served as Vice

Chairman-Asia, Chief Executive-Asia, and Managing Director of China for APCO Worldwide. He's a graduate of Yale College, with a bachelor's degree, and Princeton University with a Ph.D.

Mr. Murck, thank you for being with us. The full statements of all of the witnesses will be included as you have brought them to us, and we would ask each of the witnesses to summarize.

Mr. Murck, you may proceed.

STATEMENT OF CHRISTIAN MURCK, PRESIDENT, AMERICAN CHAMBER OF COMMERCE IN THE PEOPLE'S REPUBLIC OF CHINA

Mr. MURCK. Thank you, Mr. Chairman. It's an honor and a pleasure to appear before you. I testified once before in front of this Commission in June 2002 before your Cochairman, who I believe at the time was Chairman of the Commission. I was pleased to discover on your Web site that that testimony still survives, hidden away in one of the far recesses of the archives.

It gave me a chance to look at what I said eight years ago about intellectual property rights protection in China. One of the things I have tried to do in my current statement is review what has happened between 2002 and 2010. When we look at the enforcement regime and the legal infrastructure that supports intellectual property rights over that timeframe, we do see slow but discernible progress. That is based on a common point of view which is held in principle by both the United States and the Chinese: that intellectual property infringements are not only illegal, but undesirable, and are not a basis on which to build economic growth in a sustainable fashion.

There is a substantial bureaucratic momentum, as well as a common interest of the American and Chinese business communities behind improving intellectual property rights enforcement. We are disappointed that the progress has been so slow and there are still some notable areas which remain to be improved, particularly with respect to copyright protection of motion pictures and music, and some others. But basically we do see a way forward and we do see partners that we have been working with for some time, and some of that is outlined in my statement.

We are, at AmCham-China, turning our attention to a problem which is qualitatively different, where we do not share a common stance and a common approach. That is to a range of industrial policies often having to do with intellectual property. We are looking at the impact on our future market access and on American competitiveness.

It appears to us that many of China's industrial policies can be seen as intended to strengthen national champion companies by encouraging them to acquire or develop intellectual property, and giving them protected domestic markets in which to gain scale with the ultimate objective of being globally competitive.

In this case, the Chinese policies reflect considered, deliberate choices which are inimical to our commercial interests and which restrict both national treatment for foreign companies in the Chinese market and the development of a market economy. We were most alarmed by this development, starting late last year, by the release of a circular on indigenous innovation, which defined so-called indigenously innovated products in a manner which would exclude not only imported products, but also those of foreign-invested enterprises in China, and by the prospect that this might then be used in government procurement and State-owned enterprise procurement.

Since then, there has been a very active dialogue on this subject and many Chinese senior leaders, including Premier Wen Jiabao last week at the World Economic Forum meeting in Tianjin, have responded that the draft regulations or the 2009 regulations on this subject were improperly done, they have been changed, and that there is no intent to discriminate against the products of foreign companies.

But our concerns are substantially broader than simply that one set of regulations. They go also to technology transfer issues of the kind that the Wall Street Journal cited, which is, I would emphasize, still in the planning stages and has not yet actually happened. They go to issues of standards and how standards are formulated. They go to the CCC [China Compulsory Certificate] mark and how that is conducted, and to a range of other issues, many of which are outlined in my full statement.

These are qualitatively different from the issue of simply enforcing the rights of a trademark owner, or a patent holder, or a copyright holder. The Chinese market is one not only of very large scale, but also where there is very large future potential for growth. In many cases, it is simply too important strategically for companies to think about washing our hands and withdrawing.

On the other hand, it is clearly a market which is going to be very different in the future, as it is today from our own, in that there will be a large state-owned sector. We have to come to terms with that fact and figure out what we can do to negotiate a mutually beneficial relationship between our economy and the Chinese economy in order to realize the benefit of the synergies and the growth potential which we think are there.

Some of the suggestions that we might think about are included in my statement. I will just say that the Congress—that is, the Senate Finance Committee—did a very useful thing by encouraging or requesting the ITC [U.S. International Trade Commission] to launch an investigation on this subject. We have supported that by arranging for our members to be interviewed by the Commission. But I think much more will have to be done to develop a broad strategy, both for the U.S. Government, and also for U.S. companies, about how to respond to both the potential, and also the competitive issues that we will face in the future.

Some of the answer is in broader public sector/private sector partnerships, such as the aviation and energy programs that we are engaged in with support of the TDA [U.S. Trade and Development Agency]. Some of it is in better export promotion and strengthening the National Export Initiative. Some of it is in stronger action at the World Trade Organization, with respect to good cases have recently been brought by USTR, and a good deal of it lies in strengthening our own competitiveness in general.

Much of our future is in our own hands; it doesn't depend on what China, or anybody else, does. I have in mind here our tax structure, our educational system, our fiscal deficit, and the whole range of other things that could be put under the category of national competitiveness.

With that, I will refer you to my full statement and look forward to your questions. Thank you.

Chairman DORGAN. Mr. Murck, thank you very much. We appreciate your testimony.

Next, we'll hear from Thea Mei Lee. Thea Mei Lee is the Deputy Chief of Staff at the AFL–CIO. Previously she worked as an international trade economist at the Economic Policy Institute in Washington, DC, and as an editor at Dollars and Cents magazine in Boston. She's the author of "A Field Guide to the Global Economy," published by the New Press. Her research projects include reports on the North American Free Trade Agreement on the impact of international trade on U.S. wage inequality in the domestic steel and textile industries. She's a graduate of Smith College and has a master's degree from the University of Michigan.

Thea, you may proceed. Thank you very much.

[The prepared statement of Mr. Murck appears in the appendix.]

STATEMENT OF THEA MEI LEE, DEPUTY CHIEF OF STAFF, AFL–CIO

Ms. LEE. Thank you so much, Mr. Chairman, Mr. Cochairman, and Senator Feinstein. It's a great pleasure to be here on behalf of the 11.5 million working men and women of the AFL–CIO to talk about this very important topic today. I think a lot of people assume that business cares about intellectual property rights [IPR] enforcement, but labor is not that interested.

In fact, IPR enforcement is very important to many AFL–CIO members, not just in the entertainment and media industries, but also in the manufacturing sector. It's important to American jobs, wages, to innovation and economic growth, consumer safety, tax revenues, and the reputation of American products.

It is also true that much of the labor movement's policy priorities with respect to China have focused on other issues, including currency manipulation, worker rights, and illegal subsidies, but the lax enforcement of IPR protections remains a key contributing factor to our lopsided trade relationship.

Both in the arts and entertainment sector, where copyrights are routinely ignored, and in the manufacturing sector, where counterfeit parts and products are rampant, billions of dollars in revenue and thousands of good jobs are at stake. There's a common theme to many of the trade tensions between the United States and China.

We've raised many issues over the years, including violations of workers' rights, workplace safety and health, consumer protections, and intellectual property rights. These are linked because they're part of a single coherent economic strategy on the part of the Chinese Government.

It's an export-led strategy, which is disrespectful of international norms and basic human protections. So, these issues are all part of the same kinds of struggles and tensions that we have with the Chinese Government. We need our government to focus on how to address these in a more effective way than has been done in the past.

Taking steps now to address the Chinese Government's flagrant violations of its international obligations with respect to IPR is crucial to setting a sustainable, long-term trajectory for our bilateral relationship. This really does have to do with the issue that Mr. Murck raised about forced technology transfer and innovation, and where the next generation of innovation happens.

If the U.S. Government doesn't take more care to ensure that American workers and American businesses can benefit from the kinds of innovation and inventions that happen here in the United States, we will feel the impact of that for generations in terms of lost American jobs.

We often hear business and government officials tout the promise of the Chinese market, and of course it is both large and fast growing, but meaningful access to that market for American producers and workers is severely undercut by IPR infringement.

If American entertainment products and software cannot sell at a reasonable price in the Chinese marketplace and if the legitimate owners of those products are not able to receive their fair share of the revenues, then the size of the Chinese market is, for all intents and purposes, a tiny fraction of what it ought to be. Similarly, American products are in direct competition with Chinese-produced counterfeits, costing jobs in third country markets, as well as in the United States of America.

Over many years, the U.S. Government has made repeated attempts to cajole, pressure, or convince the Chinese Government to improve its IPR enforcement record through the use of Special 301 cases, priority watch lists, the Joint Committee on Commerce and Trade talks, and finally, WTO cases.

Each one of these things is important because it sends a message to the Chinese Government. But overall I'd have to say it has been a long, frustrating history of trying to deal with these issues in a piecemeal fashion. We haven't really seen the kinds of results we'd like to see, as you said, Mr. Chairman, in your opening remarks, and as Mr. Levin said as well. Over all, we still have enormous violations and a failure on the part of the Chinese Government to take this issue seriously and to give it the kind of attention it deserves.

This summer, the U.S. Trade Representative filed a request for a WTO panel. That was an important case, which challenged a number of practices on the part of the Chinese Government, including the quantity and thresholds in China's criminal law that must be met in order to start criminal prosecutions or obtain criminal convictions for copyright piracy. It also contested the Chinese rules that allow IPR-infringing goods that are seized by the Chinese authorities to be released into commerce, following the removal of the fake labels. Of course, this totally undermines the whole point of removing these products from the marketplace.

The third issue that USTR raised was also an important one: a challenge to the denial of copyright protection for works that are awaiting Chinese censorship approval. Under Chinese copyright law, there is no protection for these copyright holders before the censorship approval is granted. These are all enormously important issues.

Let me just conclude by saying that the Commission has asked the question: "Will China protect intellectual property?" I believe that the answer in the end will depend on our own government's actions. We haven't really been successful to date in cajoling, or convincing, or persuading the Chinese Government to act effectively.

The real key is going to be raising the price for non-compliance so that it exceeds the gains that are currently being earned by violating the intellectual property rights norms. Until that happens, American workers and businesses will continue to pay a high price, and the Chinese Government will continue on its current shortsighted path. I look forward to your questions and I look forward to the rest of the testimony today.

Thank you very much.

Chairman DORGAN. Ms. Lee, thank you very much.

Next, we will hear from Mr. Greg Frazier, executive vice president for Worldwide Government Policy at the Motion Picture Association of America. He coordinates the development and execution of the government advocacy initiatives of the Motion Picture Association on behalf of its members. He has spent more than two decades in public service, lastly as Chief Agriculture Negotiator in the Office of the USTR, serving with the rank of ambassador. Before that, he was Chief of Staff at the U.S. Department of Agriculture from 1995 to 1999, and he has held several professional staff positions in the House of Representatives as well, and many other activities.

He is a graduate of Kansas State University, and the University of Connecticut with a master's. Mr. Frazier, thank you for being with us.

[The prepared statement of Ms. Lee and the statement of the AFL–CIO Executive Council appear in the appendix.]

STATEMENT OF GREG FRAZIER, EXECUTIVE VICE PRESIDENT FOR WORLDWIDE GOVERNMENT POLICY, MOTION PICTURE ASSOCIATION OF AMERICA

Mr. FRAZIER. Thank you, Senator. I appreciate the invitation to be here. I was listening to your opening statement and I thought: "I'm not really sure what I can add to what Senator Dorgan said." You made the comment that, with a quota of only 20 foreign films allowed into China, is there any wonder that there's a movie piracy problem there.

If you look at my statement and if you look at the comments that we and our members have made over the last couple of years, you put your finger on what we believe is the critical component to dealing with movie piracy in China.

We start out by saying—most people don't realize this—that the movie industry is a trade success story. The men and women who work in the movie industry—and it's not just in California, but it's all over the country—earn about half of their earnings from outside of the United States, so it's a real success story. There's a positive balance of trade for the U.S. movie industry in every country where it does business, including China.

The Chinese market is a real paradox. We did a study a couple of years ago and we estimated that the movie piracy rate in China was 90 percent. That means, for every 10 DVDs sold in China, 9 were pirated.

Yet, the Chinese market is one of the fastest-growing theatrical markets in the world. The member companies that I represent, that I work for, their box office revenues from 2008 to 2009 doubled in China. This was a huge increase. If you look over the last two years, it has gone up about 100 percent, so it's a growing market. There's a demand for American entertainment in China.

But if you put that in context, what they earned in 2009 in China is probably about what they will earn in the United States in the month of September. Growing market, lots of piracy.

What's the problem? If you were in Beijing and you went from Mr. Murck's office and you were to take a walk to Tiananmen Square, I think you might be able to see what the problem is.

You would leave Mr. Murck's office, and very soon you would get to the Silk Market. You would walk up to the Silk Market and somebody would come up to you and whisper, "DVDs," and shove underneath your face a fistful of all of the latest movies that just opened in the United States this past weekend. You might conclude that there were lots of U.S. films available in China, and it would be a reasonable conclusion.

If you kept walking quite a bit further, there's a mall near Tiananmen Square called Oriental Plaza mall. I would direct you to two places in that mall. On one end is an audio-visual store—two stories. On the top story is equipment, on the bottom floor, is music and films. If you are patient enough and you look hard enough, you will find the American movies. It's probably about two rows of movies. Virtually none of them are current, none of them are new movies. They're fine movies, but they're not the latest releases.

How does that square with what happened at the Silk Market? Why could I get anything I wanted at the Silk Market but I can't at the AV store?

If you went down the mall a little bit there's a cinema in there. The cinema is as modern as any cinema that you would see anywhere in Washington, DC. You might see one American film playing there.

So here is the paradox: There is an abundance of American movies in China. Unfortunately, most of them are pirated. As you said in your statement, China only permits 20 foreign films into its market every year. That's not just 20 from the United States, it's 20 from all destinations. Then there are further restrictions we face as I have summarized in my written statement on television programs and home entertainment products.

So we believe that until we can get into that market and those barriers can come down, there's no way that we can compete with the Chinese pirates. Unfortunately, as other witnesses have said and as you have indicated, the pirated products that are coming out of China are showing up all over the world. This is not just a victimless crime. It's not just American men and women who are suffering.

I'm not going to say every time we buy a pirated movie it goes to an organized crime syndicate, but the Rand Corporation released a report two years ago and it said more than likely not, when we buy a $2 DVD in the Silk Market in Beijing, that money is going to go to an organized criminal syndicate based in China, perhaps doing business all over the world.

So what do we do about that? Again, in your statement you indicated, about the basics of the law, it needs changes, it needs refinements here and there. But the real problem, we believe, as you indicated, is lack of commitment from the Chinese authorities. When you were there during the Olympics it was almost impossible to find counterfeit Olympic logo material. They had an interest and a desire to protect it, and they did.

From time to time, the Chinese Government launches these campaigns, they're going to clean up this city, this district, that district. And you know, they do for a week, two weeks, three weeks. But you go back, and the material is there. There's not a sustained role, sustained commitment to address that problem.

After many years of dealing directly with the Chinese Government, dealing with the U.S. Government, the companies that I work for decided they needed to escalate this, so we went to the U.S. Government and we asked them to take a suit against China for its IPR violations and for its market access restrictions.

I am pleased to say that after thousands of hours of work by this Administration and the previous Administration, the U.S. Government prevailed at the WTO in a case that made important challenges to China's market access barriers, and, therefore, the piracy problems in China.

China has until the middle of March to come into compliance with the WTO ruling against it in the market access case. We believe that this is a critical time period on how China comes into compliance and what the future is, both in terms of our ability to grow that market and which we believe will go hand-in-hand with dealing with the piracy problem.

I guess I would close by saying that, the U.S.-Chinese relationship is complicated and there are many things at play, and movies are just one aspect. I also know you have very busy schedules, and so I appreciate you holding this hearing now during this busy time.

At the same time all three of you and your colleagues meet with Chinese officials all the time. Senator Feinstein talked about how she's been going there for over 30 years and meets with people, and she is respected and known there. The extent to which you also have those meetings, the extent to which you engage with Chinese officials, don't forget to mention how important the market access barriers are to the growth of the U.S. film industry in the China market. Coming from the U.S. Congress, it carries a lot of import, it carries a lot of weight. The few words that you can talk about intellectual property problems, the market access problems, believe me, will go a long way and will be greatly appreciated by the companies that I work for and the men and women in the American film community. Thank you.

Chairman DORGAN. Mr. Frazier, thank you very much for the testimony. We appreciate your being here.

Finally, we will hear from Richard Suttmeier, Professor of Political Science, Emeritus, at the University of Oregon. He has written widely on science and technology development issues in China. His current research includes an NSF-supported study of the role of science and technology in U.S.-China relations, the role of technical standards in China's technology policy, and the Chinese approaches to the management of technological risks. He is well-published and we're very pleased that he has come to join us today.

Mr. Suttmeier, you may proceed.

[The prepared statement of Mr. Frazier appears in the appendix.]

STATEMENT OF RICHARD P. SUTTMEIER, PROFESSOR OF POLITICAL SCIENCE, EMERITUS, UNIVERSITY OF OREGON

Mr. SUTTMEIER. Thank you very much, Mr. Chairman. I appreciate the invitation to join you here.

I have about six points I'll try to make, very briefly. The first one, is that I think it is useful to always remember that this issue is occurring in a context where we have a global economy, but not really a global consensus on norms affecting intellectual property systems. That is true, I think, with regard both to the efficiency of intellectual property issues and intellectual property arrangements, and it is also true, I think, with regard, especially when we talk about the third world, to questions about fairness of the existing intellectual property regulations and institutions.

Second, I think it is also useful to remember that, in China, this IP question manifests itself in somewhat different ways depending on the type of intellectual property you're talking about, whether it's patents, whether it's trademarks, whether it's copyrights. Different actors in China get involved in developing regulations and enforcement, and I think that that effects very much the way—we need to sort of parse out what the different types of IP issues are at different times.

I would add that also pertains to industry, and I think it also increasingly pertains to the question of Chinese innovators as rights claimants. So if we begin to look at some fields of Chinese innovative activity we see certain kinds of patterns, and in other fields we see other kinds of patterns.

Third, there clearly are changes in Chinese thinking, as you have heard already. I think it is worth keeping in mind comparative experience here; China is not the first developing country that has had serious IPR infringement problems, although it is clearly a very special case, as we all know.

But one of the things that comparative experience suggests is that as we begin to have a community of Chinese innovators in China, they begin to develop an interest in stronger IP protection. I think we're beginning to see that in China and that is true at the level of individuals and individual companies, but also is manifested in the state itself.

Now, I come to all this as a person who looks at larger industrial policy, and science and technology policy questions. To reinforce what Mr. Murck has said, the landscape is changing in China very quickly with regard to the role of intellectual property in the Chinese economy. With the launching of the big Medium- to Long-term Plan for science and technology [MLP] China's leaders are supposed to—through R&D activities and industrial policy measures—make China into an innovative society by the year 2020. This is where the indigenous innovation idea comes from. I address that a bit more in my written submission.

But I think it's important to recognize that central to this whole national effort, which has really become a very important part of Chinese public policy, is to make China a creator, a producer of IP. I think that the government understands very well that it cannot realize its objectives if, in fact, we have a deeply flawed intellectual property rights protection system.

Now, that's not to say that there are not very serious abuses, as you have heard, but I do think that it is important to try to get a sense of the context of that plan, because one of the things it's doing, is producing a whole series of incentives to make Chinese research institutes, universities, and especially companies more innovative. The policy is being operationalized by measuring IP output of one sort or another, whether it be professional papers from universities or patents from universities, research institutes, and companies.

So people in the innovation system face strong performance measures and strong incentives to perform. The New York Times last week carried an interesting piece about China being a society preoccupied with testing in its educational system, with some saying how our students would do better if there was more testing. Well, testing is a reality for Chinese enterprises, for research institutes, and so forth. They do regularly face evaluation and one of the critical performance measures is IP output, especially numbers of patents.

Now, one of the consequences of that is that we have seen an explosion of patenting, many of which can legitimately be regarded as "junk patents." But this is a new dynamic element that affects the whole technology transfer issue, the government procurement question, et cetera, because what the government is trying to do is to make Chinese enterprises successful IP producers. They are taking a variety of measures to do that, some of which I think we will all agree are ill-advised, and some of which, as Mr. Murck has pointed out, the Chinese are backing away from.

So let me move toward a conclusion here by asking about the relationship of the IP question to innovation. Why does China increasingly attract so many innovators from around the world? IPR supposedly is important for innovation, but at the same time we all have heard that China's IPR system is very weak. So wouldn't we expect innovators to avoid China? I raise this, in part, in the context of your interest in wind power and clean energy.

I think that this is a very important question as we think about the global economy. Technology transfer—and this goes to the forced technology transfer issue—is ultimately a business decision and has to be understood as such. But what we know about technology transfer decisions, and the role of intellectual property in innovation, is that even though there is intrinsic worth in the ideas found in IP, to capture value from that intellectual property you need other things.

David Teece, who has written very wisely about all this, has called these other things "complementary assets." So if we begin to think about the question of our future U.S. system of innovation, and the future Chinese system of innovation, I think we want to think not only about IPR and the strength of intellectual property protection, but also these complementary assets: Markets, market availability, scalability, finance, human resources, et cetera, which are very central issues for a lot of the clean technology questions.

In my submission, I quote a recent piece that addresses that; the availability of financing; the existence of growing capabilities in research and development; supportive government policies that makes scalability and market growth more likely in China. All of those things, I think, are part of the complementary assets that make innovators attracted to China.

So increasingly, I think we can talk about living in a global innovation system, or a global innovation network, where we can think about countries being nodes in that network.

Fifteen years ago, China was a fairly insignificant node as a producer of IP, and as a magnet for other innovators. China is now growing as an increasingly important node toward a "super-node" status. We have been the super-node in the past. We have been the place where creativity and innovation was possible, largely because we had the complementary assets as well as the very smart people who were attracted from around the world to come here. What we have to ask ourselves is, is China actually putting together that package now, and are we losing it? As I suggest in the paper, I think we have to think very hard about that.

Thank you.

[The prepared statement of Mr. Suttmeier appears in the appendix.]

Chairman DORGAN. Mr. Suttmeier, thank you very much for the interesting testimony. I think all four of you have given us a lot of things to think about.

I don't want to over-simplify this, and there's a tendency, I think, for me and everyone to over-simplify this when we talk about our relationship with China. It's clear to me that the trade deficit we have is not sustainable, it's clear to me that we operate on different planes with different strategies.

China has an export strategy. It wishes to maximize its exports, use its natural—I shouldn't say natural, use its political—advantages of lower wages and various things to be able to be attractive in foreign markets, while at the same time limiting foreign exports to the Chinese marketplace.

Mr. Murck, you heard me quote the Wall Street Journal article entitled, "China Spooks Auto Makers," and the portion says, "The draft"—they're talking about the Chinese Government draft—suggests the government could compel foreign automakers that want to produce electric vehicles in China to share critical technologies by requiring the companies to enter joint ventures in which they are limited only to a minority stake. Is it the case that if you would like to—let's say that you have an electric car strategy and you've got technology and you want to produce in China, perhaps for sale in the Chinese marketplace, and you want to start a company in China, would you be able to start a company as an American businessman and own, let's say, 51 percent of that company?

Mr. MURCK. The answer to your question is no. You would be limited to a 50/50 joint venture, which is the one, for example, that General Motors has now. In that context, General Motors controls the technology and has management control of the joint venture, and I think most people would argue that a significant portion of the value of that company today lies in the fact that they have a leading position in what is now the largest automobile market in the world. If you drive around Beijing in a Buick, which I do, very proudly, you will see lots and lots of other Buicks.

Chairman DORGAN. Let me ask you——

Mr. MURCK [continuing]. Now, the thing that's really interesting about the article, which is a report of a draft regulation, not something which has actually happened, is the assertion that the Chinese Government is considering a policy of allowing only a 49-percent foreign interest in a joint venture for these cars based on new technologies. That would imply that control of the technology and management would rest with the local party. That would certainly be an issue and that is precisely why the Wall Street Journal, and I think anybody else who sees this report, would be alarmed by it.

Chairman DORGAN. But outside of the General Motors example, it is routine, it seems to me, for China to require that the Chinese, in these circumstances, would have controlling interest. American companies would be allowed to own 49 percent of an enterprise.

Ms. Lee, if that were the case in our country and we said, you know what, if you want to come over here and do some business, we are sorry, you can't do that unless you retain only a minority ownership here in the United States, would people say, what are you doing? I mean, that violates everything we understand about free, fair, and open trade. Wouldn't that be the response?

Ms. LEE. I think there are a lot of things that the Chinese Government does that we would find either odd or problematic here in the United States. Certainly the basic principles that China agreed to when it joined the World Trade Organization, of most favored nation, right of national treatment, and so on, are things that are pretty routinely violated by the Chinese Government.

Chairman DORGAN. Mr. Frazier, how did we get to the number of 20? Who was it that sat in a trade negotiation and said to the Chinese, "Okay, you are right, we have a very big trade deficit with you, we need to sell you more, so you can go from 12 movies a year to 20 movies a year?" Good for us! Let's go have a big dinner and celebrate this success. Who was it on our side of the table?

Mr. FRAZIER. Senator, I don't know. I don't know who did it.

Chairman DORGAN. Well, you worked for USTR. Not necessarily then, but there had to have been someone who, out of some understanding that it was in somebody's interest to agree to 20 movies. Is that correct?

Mr. FRAZIER. You're absolutely correct.

Chairman DORGAN. Somebody signed up to that.

Mr. FRAZIER. Somebody signed up to it. The only logic I have for that number is it doubled it. The old quota was 10.

Chairman DORGAN. I understand that doubled. I thought it went from 12 to 20, but okay, so it doubled. But my understanding also is what I thought was born of ignorance at the time, someone on our behalf sat at a table and negotiated and said, okay, in bilateral automobile trade, once we are phased in completely on bilateral automobile trade, we will say to China, "It will be all right for you to impose a 25-percent tariff when it's fully phased in on U.S. automobiles shipped to China to be sold in your marketplace, and we will impose only a 2.5-percent tariff on Chinese vehicles sold in our place."

Now, China is ramping up an automobile export industry, we know. With a country with whom we have a very large trade deficit, we've said it will be okay if you have a 10:1 advantage in tariffs. Someone had to have decided, on one part of the table, wearing a U.S.A. jersey, negotiating on behalf of our country, yes, that's in our interest. I've always tried to find out, who are these people?

Mr. FRAZIER. I don't know. I don't know. I was there at the time, but I had charge of the agriculture portfolio, so I can only speak to some of the agricultural issues.

Chairman DORGAN. All right. What should we do with respect to movies? Why should we believe, just to use movies as an example— there are a lot of products out there, but movies are an American success story.

Mr. FRAZIER. Right.

Chairman DORGAN. What should we expect of the Chinese with respect to the allowing of importation of U.S. movies? Should we have no limitation? Do we limit Chinese movies into the United States?

Mr. FRAZIER. No.

Chairman DORGAN. No. And should we expect that China would not limit the import of U.S. movies to China?

Mr. FRAZIER. Well, in an ideal world, yes, that's what we would expect. As I indicated, this is a growing market for the U.S. industry. The box office has doubled in one year; it has gone up by 150 percent in three years. It is not just Americans, American companies and American men and women who are profiting from that.

It's the cinema owners in China, it's the people who work there, the people who provide the concessions, the people who provide the promotion, the advertisement. So there's a growing domestic industry that's profiting from the creative work of American men and women in the American film community. We see a classic win-win situation. If we can put more movies there, not only are we going to benefit, but the Chinese are going to benefit. But it's a tough road, I'll tell you.

Chairman DORGAN. I think we have lower expectations than we should of the Chinese as trade partners, and I think we ought to change that some. I'm not interested in a trade war, but I am interested in making sure we have mutually beneficial trading relationships. I don't think that is now the case with China.

Mr. Suttmeier, you made some interesting points about innovations and innovators, and so one of the dilemmas we have had is that while it may be the case that China is birthing a whole new cadre of people creating intellectual property at home and so on, it's also the case in many circumstances they've determined it is much easier just to steal it.

In the first book I wrote, I pointed out that the reports existed that the Chinese, when Viagra came out, simply re engineered Viagra and sold it in China of their own volition. They didn't need to buy it or import it, they just reengineered it and sold it. That goes on all the time, doesn't it?

Mr. SUTTMEIER. It does go on, Mr. Chairman. But I think what we're seeing, is a growing intolerance of the high level of dependence on foreign technology. That's what I think is behind all of this. The fact that it exists and the dependence comes through illicit forms, as well as quite legal forms, is, I think, what's troubling to the Chinese because what they see is that those who control the IP actually then controls the higher value-added activities of all kinds of economic activities.

So what we're seeing is a push from the technical community now backed by senior political leadership, to change that balance. But you're absolutely right. One of the great problems that the research community faces in China is that industrial enterprises, people who are making things, whether it be Viagra or something else, have a very strong bias toward foreign technology. So one of the things that people are trying to do, is to change that bias and change the balance somewhat.

Chairman DORGAN. Mr. Murck, one of the things that I note in this country is that whenever we raise the question of unfair trade, shipping of American jobs overseas as a result of unfair advantage, closed markets, and so on, we are referred to as "protectionist," some say "isolationists," "xenophobic stooges who just don't get it." It's a new world order. We need to be able to compete.

You made a point earlier that I fully agree with. There are a lot of things we need to do in our own country to get our house in order: Fiscal policy, education policy, and so on. But even if we have done all of that and we were at a new plateau, having done everything we could do to set ourselves up as being extraordinarily competitive, when we are trading with a country that does not protect intellectual property rights and has a managed trade strategy of saying we intend to run a very large trade surplus with you, we intend that you be our cash cow for hard currency needs, and we're going to do it year, after year, after year as long as you're willing to allow that, and as long as those who are critical in your country are called isolationists or protectionists, nothing is going to change in your country.

That brings me to the Chamber of Commerce. Mr. Donohue and others would take a listen to something I say and they'd say, well, shame on you, that's anti-business. I happen to think that an American business man or woman, today, producing a product that says, "Made in America," in Pittsburgh or Bismarck, wanting to compete internationally and wanting to have a fair opportunity to compete internationally, has a very large gripe with this country, with the Chamber, and others who have supported a trade strategy that I think undermines our own economic interests.

It's one thing for us not to be able to compete when the competition is fair. It's another thing to tie our hands behind our back and then say "compete." We could do that after the second World War with anybody and beat them; we were bigger, better, stronger. We had the most. But these days, things have changed.

So I mentioned the Chamber. The American Chamber of Commerce in these countries is very important. They have a very important role. On my first visit to Vietnam, the American Chamber of Commerce in Vietnam said something I'll never forget. They said, "You know what we need in Vietnam?" This was a time when it was coming out into a market system with a Communist government. "We need more government." I said, "Really?" They said,

"Yes. You can only do business when you can enforce contracts, when you have administrative practices." It is absolutely true, that is the case.

So give me your perspective, Mr. Murck. I'm sorry for the lengthy question. Give me your perspective of what we can, and should, expect on behalf of American businesses producing here today, trying to compete in an international marketplace with the support of the Chamber of Commerce.

Mr. MURCK. Well, thank you very much, Mr. Chairman, for that question. I think this would be a good time to point out that the American Chamber of Commerce in China is an independent organization, supported by our members on the ground, and we have no relationship other than a loose affiliation as a member with the U.S. Chamber of Commerce or Mr. Donohue. I count him among those who usually meet with me when he comes to Beijing, but I would say my influence on his thinking and his ideas, and those of the Chamber, is quite limited.

I would also just like to circle back before responding directly to your question to the Viagra issue. You might be interested to know that the counterfeiters, at the time when Viagra was widely copied in China, engaged in all kinds of brand extension efforts, including soft drinks that were laced with Viagra, and my favorite is a hot dog that was also laced with Viagra. But at the end of day——

Chairman DORGAN. That was answering a question I hadn't asked, Mr. Murck.

Mr. MURCK. Yes. I give you that for future use.

Chairman DORGAN. Thank you.

Mr. MURCK. At the end of the day, Pfizer won its case and it is now purely an enforcement issue. That was one of the first major IPR cases contested vigorously. The clear winner of that case was Pfizer, so that is actually a positive example for IPR protection.

With respect to the broader question of what you can expect from people like ourselves or the business community in general, I do think it is important that more American companies begin to compete actively in global markets. I do think there is more that we can do to make that possible in terms of export promotion and assistance of all kinds, and I've suggested in my statement some of the things of that sort. The German Government does a better job, for example.

In terms of what we do with respect to our trade policy views, we always try to express them in terms of American national interest. I do firmly believe that the global competitiveness of American companies is in the national interest of the United States, including our ability to compete in China. For that reason, I'm really not too apologetic about the many policy statements that have come out of the American Chamber of Commerce in China over the last 10 years. Mr. Donohue can defend himself without any assistance from me.

In terms of the strategy that the U.S. Government ought to adopt going forward, I would just like to associate myself with Professor Suttmeier's statement, which I think is very interesting and very sophisticated, and which poses the problem that we face very clearly.

The industrial policy issue and the way in which it draws on IPR is a qualitatively different situation than the enforcement issue that we've been struggling with over the last 10 or 15 years, and we need to have a better approach to how we are going to deal with the Chinese Government. We have to convince them, on the basis of mutual benefit, to change the way in which they're dealing with us.

One aspect of that is prioritizing the protracted, but recently begun, negotiations to enter the government procurement agreement at the WTO. This is enormously important to us because China has a very large government sector, and there are a number of other things, such as a bilateral investment treaty, that would be other pieces of developing a new and broader framework for the way in which we work with the Chinese in the future.

They have explicitly stated that their goal is to bring their global trade account into balance. So far, year-to-date, they're about 20 percent less in terms of their global surplus than they were a year ago, and a year ago it was less than 2008. I think there is very good reason to believe that this will happen, but that doesn't mean the bilateral trade balance will come into balance. This is something that will continue to require very careful attention on your part and on the part of the business community. Thank you.

Chairman DORGAN. Mr. Murck, thank you very much. I fear that I have intruded on Congressman Levin's time.

Congressman Levin, take as much time as you wish.

Representative LEVIN. I will take just a couple of minutes because I don't think there's any disagreement about the importance of our relationship. Sometimes it is misstated that there is a difference of opinion about the importance. Indeed, it is so important, in part because it is so large, and therefore, it is so complex. I have been trying to figure out, as the four of you testified: What are the differences in emphases and nuances? That isn't always easy to figure out. There are differences in emphases among the four of you and differences in nuances.

So I'm not sure where to begin. I will ask that my statement be placed in the record, Mr. Chairman.

Chairman DORGAN. Without objection.

[The prepared statement of Representative Levin appears in the appendix.]

Representative LEVIN. So let me just say this. I think it's clear that China has a strategy I think it's fairly clear, what its strategy is. You have outlined what the goals are. I think, though, there are some changes. I think you can describe fairly well what the strategy basically is. You mentioned about a certain level of technology by a certain given date. They have other goals, and I think their own strategy to achieve those goals.

I think the problem is that our country hasn't had a strategy. Therefore, we tend to kind of do it piece by piece, and it's hard to fit the pieces together. In some respects, we haven't had a strategy because there have been some in this town who thought we did not need one, and that essentially the best way to handle these issues is to leave them alone and they'll work themselves out.

For example, on government procurement, Professor, I think China decided it was better off not being a party to the agreement for a certain period of time. I don't think it was accidental. I think they sat down and figured out what would be best. I think they do that as to everything. It is further complicated, Mr. Murck, because a lot of the companies, American companies that do business in China, are global companies and they not only do business in China, and in many cases import to China, but also export from China. That is likely to increase.

So I just want to urge, I think the importance of this hearing is to underline the need for our country to develop a strategy as to how we're going to handle a burgeoning development, a country that has become so important economically, that has different structures and different interests than we do.

So when we talk about something that's mutually beneficial, I think we have to understand, that, as true in all kinds of competition, there will not always be answers that are immediately thought to be beneficial. That makes it more difficult to work them out. But our country had better put together a strategy as to how we're going to handle this relationship. Those who thought we could not have one, I think, or that it had to be outside of a larger structure, I think they were basically wrong.

But the problem is, within this structure that now exists, the problems remain so compelling, for example, movies. You bring your perspective. You work with them. You tell the typical American citizen that China has complete access, while we have very limited, and that when we have access it's essentially overcome by pirated product. They have to ask themselves, how can this be? The same is true increasingly—and you referred to this, Mr. Murck—in the industrial sector. I thought it was excellent that GM—I was there before the plant was even built, and I'm glad General Motors went there.

However, it creates problems as well as profit. When you have increasing counterfeiting of auto parts and you're likely to have, as a result of that proliferation of American enterprise in China, an increasing number of parts produced in China that come here that are counterfeited and compete with American-made products, I don't think it is workable that we not have some kind of a strategy.

So maybe I won't ask questions, because I think the nuances in your testimony really indicate the need for us to work out within this country how we're going to handle this increasing trade with, and competition from, China. If, today, I asked any of you, what is our strategy, I think you would be somewhat hard pressed to indicate really what it is. It varies from industry to industry.

I will just finish with this. I was at a solar plant in Michigan. It is three or four football fields long. They make solar panels. The person who manages it, who is the opposite of a xenophobe, took me aside after I had been through it and said, unless this country has a strategy in this renewable energy field, it is likely, in five years, every single solar panel installed in the United States will come from China, and not for just one reason. Currency is one, the subsidization by the Chinese, another. It may well be that some American companies will have an interest in those solar panel plants in China, but this fellow tells me that all of the workers in that company in Michigan, in five years, are likely to be out of work, and our company out of business, if this country does not get together itself.

Then I went to another place that produces a very important ingredient in high technology, also in Michigan. This is a huge plant, with endless pipes that I can't begin to understand. The CEO says to me—he's the CEO—that unless we get ourselves together, it's unlikely, over a period of time, that that plant can survive.

So, I left there saying to myself, we'd better get our heads together and not call each other labels if we have differences, and not use some of the old shibboleths, and not have deep cleavages before we even start to talk in this country. There is an urgency in terms of our relationship with China economically, and also, if I might close, in terms of human rights.

This Commission has been invaluable in its creation and its work on human rights. I think the Chinese need to expect that we will not only insist on measures so that they abide by their commitments that were made when they went into the WTO, but also that we will continue to have an interest in the liberties of people in China.

So I think this has been, Mr. Chairman, a really useful hearing and I salute—if I might say so, I'm a bit biased, I agree—the work of the Commission and its staff over these years since the creation of the Commission. It was part of PNTR. So, thank you very much.

Chairman DORGAN. Congressman Levin, thank you very much. I think the point you made that is so important, is this country and China will have a very important bilateral relationship. The question is, will it be mutually beneficial? I think most of the witnesses have indicated that there is movement in China. I think Senator Feinstein put it pretty well. Just go back 30 years and see what existed then and see what exists now, and there's movement. You can make a pretty strong case that things are better in China.

But you also indicated there is some urgency to address these trade imbalances and the trade relationship with China. I agree with that. If we don't push the requirement to address them, we will, in 5 years, 10 years, and 15 years, see this drag on and on and on.

Ms. Lee, tell me how it is that China can largely say to an American company, yes, you can produce over here, in fact, we would insist that you produce over here. You make something that we want to buy and you buy our products, China would say to us, so we have something that we want to buy from you. But in order to do that, we want your manufacturer to move to China and make it in China, and by the way, when you do, you are only able to own 49 percent of the company. Does that violate all kinds of WTO rules?

Representative LEVIN. Mr. Chairman, if you'll excuse me. I hate to leave, especially at this moment, but I think I have to go to another appointment. So, I will have others tell me the answer to this salient question.

Chairman DORGAN. All right.

Representative LEVIN. Thank you. Thank you so much.

Chairman DORGAN. Congressman Levin, thank you very much.

Let me, by consent, also ask that the full statement of Senator Carl Levin from the State of Michigan be included in the hearing record at this point.

[The prepared statement of Senator Levin appears in the appendix.]

Chairman DORGAN. Ms. Lee, you've had time to think about that now.

Ms. LEE. Thank you, Mr. Chairman. It's an excellent question. It's one that has been a huge problem for us and for certain unions for many years. It is illegal under many kinds of rules, but they are difficult to enforce. It's called an offset agreement, where the Chinese Government negotiates with an individual company to make a sale—for example, aircraft—and in exchange, both jobs and technology, often, are transferred to China.

It's something that sometimes the companies aren't happy about, but they feel that it's impossible for them individually to protest because if they say no, then another company from another country could accept the deal and get the sale. Of course, they really want that sale badly. I don't know how many times we've raised this issue with our government and asked them to go to the Chinese Government and negotiate and so on.

Part of the problem is that we don't have a united front among all the different governments that deal with China. Each one is afraid of losing that sale, so it becomes an issue. A lot of times these deals are made in secret. They're not explicit, they're not made public, so only the company itself knows exactly what deal was cut. It's not in their interest to publicize it widely. I think a lot of times these companies make a bad decision. They hope, well, it's not good to give away to technology on my wing production, but it's better than losing this particular sale. So it's a very short-sighted decision.

What we need, obviously, is a much more concerted, multilateral approach to this problem. To date, we haven't gotten it. Whether it's through the OECD [Organisation for Economic Co-operation and Development], whether it's through the World Trade Organization, we need all the governments to come together with a united front. We need the companies to be up front about the kinds of deals that they're being asked to make. So far, we haven't had that kind of cooperation. It's been very frustrating for us and it costs us a lot of good jobs, and a lot of technology.

Chairman DORGAN. Mr. Murck, you represent the American Chamber. And thank you for clarify all of the relationships. My mentioning Mr. Donohue, I don't mean that in an unflattering light. He has his own view of issues and he pursues them very vigorously. But having said that, I hear from businesses who say, in order to sell into China we had to move our production to China, accept a minority ownership, and then we lost control of our intellectual property and they're very upset about that.

I say, why don't you speak of that publicly? They say, we don't dare. We don't dare speak of that publicly. We would never be able to do any business with China in the future. So, do you hear some of those same stories, Mr. Murck? I mean, it's probably understandable why people in that situation—if they're going to sell into China, they've got to accept the dictums of the Chinese Government, and that's the way it is. They're certainly not going to want to complain publicly about it or they won't be selling there at all.

Mr. MURCK. I think there are a couple of points that I would make. First of all, in the 1980s, after the Chinese economy began to be open in a serious way to foreign investment, which began only in 1979, the requirement at the time was that every foreign company had to joint venture. One hundred percent of them were joint ventures. That requirement has gradually been relaxed. When China entered the WTO, there are only a few sectors in which the joint venture requirement was maintained. One of them is automobiles, and there are some others. There are some that are totally closed to foreign investment even today, for example, upstream oil and natural gas production.

Chairman DORGAN. Was that in contravention of WTO or was that negotiated?

Mr. MURCK. That was negotiated at the time.

Chairman DORGAN. All right.

Mr. MURCK. The vast majority of our members are in China on a wholly foreign-owned basis, and it's relatively unusual nowadays for a joint venture to be established, except in those sectors which continue to be restrictive and which were negotiated as part of China's WTO accession. So I don't usually hear the complaint that you mentioned in exactly that form.

However, the broader issue is absolutely there, that if you come to China and you bring your intellectual property into the market, it is necessary to take a very determined look at how to protect that IPR. There is now an emerging set of best practices which are outlined in my full statement which enables people to do that to a large extent, but it's still one of the major risks of coming into this market and something that everyone has to continue to focus on.

With respect to technology transfer, these are always individual commercial decisions. I think companies need to understand that when they transfer technology today they are not only winning an immediate contract, but they may also be nurturing a future global competitor. The view that people take of entering into these technology contracts, as a result, has changed somewhat in the last few years. This is a new situation which we all have to face going forward.

I would just say also that I think both myself and my colleagues on this panel would agree with Cochairman Levin's remark, that we don't really have a strategy and we need one. We are very interested in thinking about this, working with some other trade association partners. I know the U.S. Government is working on this as well, and hearings like this are a step in that direction.

Chairman DORGAN. Just two more questions, Mr. Frazier, and then I want to ask Mr. Suttmeier a question. Mr. Frazier, it seems to me key to many of these issues is to not only negotiate good trade agreements, but also have the capability to enforce them.

One of my significant complaints about our trade laws in this country and the whole trade issue, is we tend to think, if we negotiate a conclusion in a trade agreement, and negotiators have in their mindset that to negotiate to an end and have an agreement is success. It's less important what's in it, if you get an agreement, that's called success. That's much easier to do than to enforce.

In fact, recently, a couple of years ago, someone was trying to gather up all of the trade agreements we had negotiated with Japan so they could get them all in writing, because they discovered they couldn't even find them, let alone enforce them. So the question is, should we not expect, with a wide range of these issues, a more effective and more aggressive enforcement mechanism in the government, and where should that be?

Mr. FRAZIER. Well, clearly. And I agree with you, the negotiator's job is to negotiate an agreement, get a deal. When I was a negotiator, one of the most important lessons I learned is, you have to know when to step away. A done deal is not necessarily a good deal, and sometimes the best deal is no deal. That was based on my experience.

Also from my experience when I was at USTR, as much time as I spent negotiating, I spent infinitely more time on the subject that you are raising: enforcement. How do I make sure that the other party is living up to its agreements? That is hard work. That is a lot harder than doing the negotiating.

My own personal bias from my background, is USTR is the place to do it. They rely on Congress for more sources, they rely on other agencies in the Executive Branch for the expertise and the help to do it. But you put your finger on it. It's a lot of work, doing the enforcement.

Chairman DORGAN. Mr. Suttmeier, you indicated that because China is nurturing innovators inside of that country, that the failure to protect intellectual property will hurt people inside of the country that have been nurtured by government policy. So we should expect and understand that China, for its own selfish reasons, will begin to tighten in these areas.

I understand the point you're making. I have very little confidence, however, that if we do nothing and our response is as it has always been, that there will be much difference moving forward on the protection of our intellectual property. You believe there will be, inevitably, improvement. Over what timeframe would you think there will be improvement sufficient so that we could expect the same kind of reasonable protections in China as we provide here?

Mr. SUTTMEIER. That may be quite some years. A different system, I think. It comes back, I think, a little bit to my very first point about whether or not you can expect the Chinese to subscribe to all of the assumptions and the norms about intellectual property that some people in this country do. But as you may know, even within this country we have a pretty wide range of views about whether our patent system is working or is it not working. It serves some industries better than other industries.

I think that kind of churn, if you will, goes on in China as well. One of the additional complications in all of this, I didn't mention, but is in my written statement, is the role of local governments and the extent to which local governments, at the provincial and sub-provincial levels, are on the same page as the national government.

So part of the enforcement problem is that we see local governments with increased authority to do something and yet they are not always doing the same thing that the central government or central policy would suggest. So it's difficult to answer your question, I think, because you're coming at it from really very different philosophical and institutional arrangements.

Chairman DORGAN. Yes. But I think in some ways it's a matter of will. The Chinese are very active, having thousands and thousands of people watching Internet traffic to try to shut off mainstream Chinese citizens from free access to the Internet. Right? That's a matter of will. They've decided, that's what we're going to do.

Mr. Frazier made the point that when the Chinese Government owned as their own possession the logo for the Chinese Olympics, they were very tough in shutting down, to the extent they could, counterfeits, the pennants, the cups, and the pencils, and so on that were sold. They demonstrated, it seems to me, all that I know, at that point, if they have the will to shut something down, they shut it down.

Mr. SUTTMEIER. Senator, I think one of the ways I would respond to that, is that central authority and the will that you're talking about, is really one of the scarcest commodities in China. So the question then becomes, where does that commodity get allocated, to whom, and to what kind of a problem? So, yes. I think you can repeat this in many, many different areas of public policy. When you have a very high priority item or issue, such as the Olympics, you can mobilize that attention, you can mobilize that will.

Chairman DORGAN. Yes.

Mr. SUTTMEIER. It dissipates on a regular day-to-day basis.

Chairman DORGAN. Your point is a fair point about local government versus central government. But let me just say that, sitting in your chair, we have had people who have testified before this Commission who have spent years and years in Chinese prisons because of a national will and a central government that made decisions that reached way out into the villages, into rural areas. Where this national government in China wishes to affect behavior, it does. We know that because we know the names of people sitting in prison today because they spoke freely, because they went on the Internet, or did one thing or another.

I think it is giving a pass to the central government to suggest that someone else might do something they're not aware of. It's a big old country. But my point is, when we have a trade relationship with China—and our relationship is one of engagement—we've long ago decided the best way to address the issue of China is through constructive engagement, and constructive engagement, we believe, through trade and travel will lead China toward greater human rights. I think there is some evidence that that has been the case. It's far from perfect, to wit, the folks that are now in prison whose names that we have, and photographs we have, for the most part.

But despite that, once we decided to engage through constructive engagement and have a trading relationship with China, and understanding China is going to be a major part of our economic future—the economic future of the world for that matter—then the question is, under what conditions do we engage? Are they fair?

What has happened, in my judgment, is China has had a very deliberate and very effective strategy, an export market strategy that exports to us and to others to the extent that they can, and then to the extent that they can, limit, as much as is possible, the import of goods from us to them. If you go to—again, in a book I wrote—a Wal-Mart store in China, go search for an American-made good, and you discover part of the problem.

The point you have brought today is very interesting, Professor, and I'm pleased that you've done that. I had not thought about this before. It is certainly the case that if China is now breeding a new group of innovators to create intellectual property in the country, they inevitably at some point are going to want to try to protect that. But if it's over a long period of time, we're going to be stuck between here and there with unsustainable trade deficits and a weakened American economy.

Mr. SUTTMEIER. If I may, Senator, briefly.

Chairman DORGAN. Yes.

Mr. SUTTMEIER. To go back to your question about, what is the timeframe, it might be useful, in fact, to think a little bit about the evolution of the IP system, starting from virtually nothing in the mid-1980s to where they are today, referencing Senator Feinstein's observations as well. You then throw into that mix the fact that this is a very different place in 2010 than it was in 1985.

I think there's a long way to go before you'll have all these vigorous and very robust innovators, but there are a lot of them beginning to emerge and I think they are not entirely happy with the conditions that are being faced, especially in things like software, but in other areas as well.

Chairman DORGAN. I thank you very much. We have been trying, on a number of occasions, mostly with respect to human rights and the issue of political prisoners in China, to shine all the spotlights in one spot. Today, we wanted to talk about the issue of intellectual property and related trade matters. I think the four of you have given us a lot of interesting information for the permanent record of this Commission to consider, and I appreciate, Mr. Murck, you coming to us from Beijing, and Mr. Suttmeier, you came from Oregon, is that correct?

Mr. SUTTMEIER. These days, only northern New York.

Chairman DORGAN. All right. Well, you didn't travel very far then. But I want to thank Thea Mei Lee and Greg Frazier. Thank you, Mr. Murck. Thanks to all of you for coming to provide testimony. We keep the records open for two weeks; if you wish to submit supplemental information you're welcome to do that.

This hearing is adjourned.

[Whereupon, at 4:00 p.m. the hearing was adjourned.]

APPENDIX

Prepared Statements

Prepared Statement of Christian Murck

SEPTEMBER 22, 2010

Mr. Chairman and Members of the Commission:

Thank you for the opportunity to testify before you on intellectual property rights in China.

I speak on behalf of the American Chamber of Commerce in China, comprising over 1,600 companies and 2,600 individuals, and representing the commercial interests of the American business community in China.

This Commission has a record of sustained attention to intellectual property rights protection in China for which we thank you. I testified before the Commission on June 6, 2002, and cited intellectual property rights as a case study of the impact of the rule of law on business. Revisiting this topic today, I will take the opportunity to comment on the progress, or the lack of it, in the past eight years, as well as new developments.

Infringement of intellectual property rights has consistently been among the top business challenges reported by our members in our annual business climate survey conducted for the past twelve years. In the 2010 survey, it ranked eighth, behind inconsistent regulatory interpretation, management level human resource constraints, obtaining licenses, protectionism, bureaucracy, unclear regulations, and lack of transparency. IPR protection was described as critically important to 25 percent of the respondents, and very important to 45 percent. 30 percent said it was slightly important or not important. You will not be surprised to hear the sectors most impacted are IT, high tech, software, research-based pharmaceuticals, entertainment, and consumer brand owners for which IPR protection is a crucial element of the business model. Least affected are service providers such as consultants, law firms, financial services, accountants and the like.

Our survey data confirms anecdotal evidence that IPR enforcement has gradually improved since 2002. In that year, 21 percent of respondents rated enforcement as totally ineffective, 63 percent as ineffective, and 16 percent as effective or very effective. In 2010, 11 percent rated enforcement as totally ineffective, 63 percent as ineffective, and 26 percent as effective or very effective. Given the attention and commitment of resources to this effort by the Chinese government, the U.S. government, and the private sector, such slow, modest improvement is a disappointment.

Nevertheless there has been significant improvement in the legal infrastructure supporting intellectual property rights.

Relevant laws are updated on a regular basis. The process takes about three years and circulation of drafts for comment is now routine.

Courts are increasingly professional and fair, especially in large cities. Enforcement of judgments against individuals and small companies is difficult, but there is adequate enforcement against large companies. Damages are growing, but still inadequate by international standards.

As a result of these improvements, litigation is now common, whereas in 2002 it was not.

The Supreme People's Court reported over 30,000 cases closed during 2009, a 29 percent increase on the prior year. Half of 2009 cases involved copyright disputes, 23 percent trademark disputes, 15 percent patents, 4 percent unfair competition, and 2.4 percent technology contracts, demonstrating the range of applicable law. A common assumption has been that once Chinese parties obtained intellectual property rights, they would seek enforcement. That is happening. In 2009, 95 percent of lawsuits involved two Chinese parties. Chinese rights holders are turning to the courts to assert their rights in large numbers.

Foreign parties litigate cautiously and they generally win. In Beijing's First Intermediate Court from 2002 to 2006, foreign parties won 60 percent of IPR cases. In Zhejiang Province, foreign plaintiffs won 95 percent of their cases from 2003-2008, and 99 percent in 2008.

One of our member companies for the first time recently filed a high profile suit against a state-owned enterprise infringer, won, and collected material damages. Though they did not recover the extent of their commercial loss, half a dozen similar companies subsequently quietly initiated negotiations to settle similar infringement situations.

While not completely satisfactory and limited by the difficulty of gathering evidence, litigation is now a much more realistic option than in 2002.

As a general matter, however, infringement is still widespread and continues to evolve in order to evade enforcement.

In my 2002 appearance before you, I suggested that an unintended consequence of WTO entry might be an increase in counterfeit exports. That has unfortunately occurred. Customs has increased inspection of outward bound containers, but is dependent on intelligence from rights holders. Recently, counterfeiters have shifted to small packages rather than container shipments, complicating the interdiction effort. The counterfeit supply chain has globalized, with distributors operating in the Middle East and Eastern Europe. The recorded country of origin of counterfeit goods entering the United States or European Union is often not China. Nevertheless, China is the known source of well over half the counterfeit goods seized at the borders of the United States and European Union.

Counterfeiting has also gone online. In one case, a single individual was operating a virtual enterprise from his home where his website listed hundreds of fake products available, and manufacturing, storage, and shipping was outsourced to dispersed companies. He is now in jail, but his business model is no doubt flourishing in the hands of others. The issue of counterfeit goods for sale through online auction or purchasing sites is well-known. Internet intermediary liability is an under-developed area of law now receiving attention.

Anti-counterfeiting enforcement now often requires investigation across both provincial borders within China and international borders.

Cooperation among international enforcement agencies continues to lag the increasing sophistication of manufacturing, distribution, and sales of counterfeit goods.

Copyright and patent infringement is equally widespread.

I will leave the subject of music and film copyrights to my colleague on this panel, except to note that a significant part of the problem is caused by the limited number of foreign films permitted to be distributed legally in China every year. This is justified by China as necessary to protect consumers, enable censorship, and protect the domestic industry. It simply cedes a large market to pirates.

China now ranks second globally in the number of personal computers shipped domestically, but 49th in revenues of international software vendors. Most of the gap is filled by pirated software. AmCham-China is particularly disappointed that despite clear regulations requiring computers to be shipped with legally licensed software, and requiring state-owned enterprises to use only legally licensed software, compliance by SOE's is still problematic. We call on the State-Owned Assets Supervision and Administration Commission to establish a credible, transparent software asset management program under which all centrally-owned SOE's will certify annually under audit that all software on their computers, including operating systems and applications software, is properly licensed.

Over time best practices have emerged with respect to protecting intellectual property in China. An effective strategy usually includes:

- Registration of trademarks, patents, and copyrights so that they are effective in China;
- Strong internal and technical controls, including access limitations to intellectual property, control of packaging, IP audits, limits on subcontracting, etc.;
- Contracts with employees, distributors, suppliers and customers that include intellectual property provisions;
- Monitoring use of IPR by employees, competitors, suppliers, and partners;
- An enforcement strategy including use of investigation firms to gather evidence, supporting enforcement agencies in administrative and criminal cases, and private litigation; and
- Active, targeted engagement with enforcement agencies at central, provincial and local levels, both as an individual company and through industry associations.

Companies with a presence on the ground and the revenue scale that justifies an active, multi-faceted effort can control the commercial impact of infringement. However, smaller firms or those without an active presence in China are seriously disadvantaged.

In the past eight years, the U.S. and Chinese governments have devoted time and effort to this situation.

There is a particularly productive engagement between the U.S. Patent and Trademark Office and the State Intellectual Property Office. Last week, for example, a patent workshop was held in Beijing organized by USPTO, SIPO, and the U.S. Chamber of Commerce. Among the topics covered were:

- The national security review required by the Patent Law when patents registered in China are licensed abroad;

- Design and utility model patents, which meet a lower standard of invention and are often unexamined, making them a means of registering other's technology;
- Patent disclosure requirements, especially the requirement that direct and indirect genetic resources be disclosed on any biotech patent;
- Statutory damages;
- Compulsory licensing (we hope China will continue to construe the grounds narrowly and avoid using compulsory licensing);
- Invention remuneration (the issue is differences between the national patent law and some provincial regulations that has led to legal uncertainty);
- Software patents

The same delegation participated this week in a workshop on bad faith trademark filings with Chinese, European, and Japanese representatives to review the law, procedural challenges and best practices to deter such filings.

These topics give a good sense of the range of subjects under active technical discussion.

Improving intellectual property rights protection has also been a major priority of the U.S. Embassy in Beijing, represented by the presence of an IPR Attaché, the annual Ambassadors IPR roundtable, and many other programs.

USTR and the Department of Commerce are actively engaged through the Joint Commission on Commerce and Trade, and its IPR Working Group.

The business community is well-linked to all of these ongoing efforts.

Our progress since 2002 can be described as a "three yards and a cloud of dust" offense, slowly grinding our way forward. It isn't very exciting, but we're better off than we were and we see a path toward the future. There is both bureaucratic momentum and the common interest of the Chinese and foreign business communities in improving IPR enforcement.

Our attention at AmCham-China and in the foreign business community in China at large is shifting from enforcement to a new consideration: the impact on our market access and American competitiveness of Chinese industrial policies explicitly intended to strengthen national champion companies by encouraging them to acquire or develop intellectual property, giving them protected domestic markets in which to gain scale, and planning that they will then be globally competitive.

I discussed this issue earlier this year in testimony at the International Trade Commission on June 15 and at the Ways and Means Committee on June 16.

As the recovery from global economic crisis continues, China is embarking on rebalancing its growth model to move back to a balanced trade account and shift toward domestic demand as the driver of economic growth. At the same time, the economy is being restructured to be more efficient in its use of energy, natural resources, and capital. Significant investments are being made in health care and education. Wages, especially manufacturing wages, are growing strongly after a long period of stagnation. Part of China's strategy to adjust to new circumstances is to move its industrial sector up the value-added curve by encouraging the development of intellectual property through research and development, technology transfer, and adaptation of acquired technologies.

Late last year, we and others were alarmed by the release of policies that appeared designed to exclude imported products and the products of foreign-invested enterprises from catalogues of products certified as the result of "indigenous innovation", with the likelihood that such catalogues would be used in government and SOE procurement. In response to comments from many quarters, the Chinese government entered into a serious dialogue. The Ministry of Science and Technology has removed the most egregious aspects of the 2009 regulations from the 2010 draft. Premier Wen Jiabao on several occasions, most recently earlier this month at the World Economic Forum meeting in Tianjin, has directly stated that foreign-invested enterprises in China are regarded as Chinese enterprises and will not be discriminated against. These are welcome statements, but it is important to recognize that there are broader concerns about the future direction of Chinese policy and the market access of foreign companies.

Our concerns include:

- Import substitution policies such as the Guiding Catalogues of Major Indigenous Innovation Technologies and Equipment of 2009, which specifies import substitution as a goal.
- The Government Procurement Law directly discourages procurement of imported products. China is not a member of the WTO Government Procurement Agreement and its first offer to join was not commercially meaningful; a second offer made in July was a modest improvement, but much work remains to be done.

- Standardization mandates such as the Ministry of Industry and Information Technology requirement that the Chinese WLAN Authentication and Privacy Infrastructure (WAPI) standard be included with any Wi-Fi enabled mobile device. Since this standard has not been commercially accepted anywhere, including in China, this mandate is purely rent-seeking.
- The 2008 Patent Law expanded the grounds for compulsory licensing, though China has not yet used them. It also requires foreign companies in China to submit to a review by Chinese authorities of whether a patent originated in China "relates to the security or vital interests of the State", including "the substantial economic interest of the State", before it can be exported.
- The Standardization Administration of China is developing standards rules that could lead to compulsory licensing or licensing on non-commercial terms of foreign technologies used in "mandatory national standards", and possible anti-trust consequences for refusal to comply.
- Exclusion of representatives of foreign-invested enterprises from participating in and/or voting in China's standards setting committees.
- Exemptions from infringement in the patent law and drug registration rules for "research" and "non-commercial use" and for research for the purpose of producing generic pharmaceuticals. These facilitate stockpiling of infringing products, reverse engineering, and generic competition with innovative pharmaceutical companies in advance of patent expiration.
- Technology transfer on terms favorable to the Chinese party required to win necessary government approval for large contracts.
- Selective enforcement of the Anti-Monopoly Law, which rarely reviews transactions involving no foreign party.
- Bid specifications that favor local producers, for example in the wind power sector.
- The Multi-level Protection Scheme requiring that technology infrastructure in key sectors runs on domestic hardware and software where possible. This is already reducing foreign market access in the banking sector.
- Sectoral restructuring policies that generally involve consolidation driven by state-owned enterprise expansion as the expense of the private sector, for example, in the coal industry and also in the rare earths industry.

These problems are qualitatively different from inadequate enforcement of intellectual property rights. We agree in principle that IPR infringement is illegal, undesirable, and a drag on China's development. We are working together toward solutions of a wide range of genuine practical difficulties to improve enforcement. We might wish that there were stronger political will on the Chinese side, or that better enforcement would be given a higher priority, and they might wish we were more patient, but we share a basic stance.

The industrial policy issues listed above, however, reflect considered, deliberate policy choices inimical to our commercial interests that restrict both national treatment and development of a market economy.

The underlying problem exposed by these policies is the very different regulatory and economic systems of our two countries. In China, the government's regulatory and planning bodies, state-owned enterprises, and the institutions of the Party all play a large role in managing the society and the economy. Only the first of these have counterparts in the United States and their role is much different. How should we relate to an economy and a market driven to a large extent by industrial policy?

SOE's can be simultaneously customers, suppliers, partners, and competitors. The leaders of major SOE's are ministerial level officials, who often hold senior Party office as Central Committee members or alternate members. Yet given the size and growth potential of China's markets for many products, it is strategically necessary to compete successfully there in order to be a global leader. We cannot throw up our hands and abandon the market because of its differences with our. Of course, the same is also true for Chinese enterprises with respect to the U.S., EU, and Japanese markets, where Chinese home market advantages often turn into disadvantages.

In our active discussions with the Chinese government and media, we often make the fundamental points that restricting competition stifles innovation, and that protected markets based on unique domestic standards prevent local firms from succeeding in global markets based on harmonized international standards. We recognize there is a vigorous policy debate within China, with many unresolved issues.

In thinking about the future, the American Chamber of Commerce in China starts with the premise that it is realistic to think in terms of $3 trillion long-term goals:

(1) Increasing US exports to China from $80 billion to $1 trillion annually;

(2) Increasing the revenues of US firms producing goods and services in China for the Chinese market from approximately $100 billion to $1 trillion annually; and

(3) Welcoming cumulative foreign direct investment from China in the United States of $1 trillion. Just as Japanese capital has contributed to job creation and economic development in the United States, so too can Chinese direct investment, giving the investors a deeper interest in our mutual prosperity and broader exposure to our market norms.

If we think in terms of building on the synergy between the U.S. and Chinese economies on this scale, what must be done?

We suggest the following:

• We need to understand better China's policy framework. Based on that understanding, we can better define the goals of our trade negotiators and private companies. For this reason, we have supported the investigation of the International Trade Commission now underway by arranging for member companies to be interviewed. We look forward to the ITC reports and hope that they will provide useful strategic input for all parties. We hope to contribute to an ongoing strategic discussion of U.S. options.

• We support the National Export Initiative, noting that China is our third largest and fastest growing export market.

• In support of the NEI, we support increased funding for the Trade Development Administration. AmCham-China participates in two private sector/public sector partnerships in aviation and energy that bring together Chinese and U.S. government agencies with American and Chinese enterprises in capacity-building programs partially funded with seed money from TDA. These are generating business opportunities as well as institutional and personal relationships that will be of last benefit to both countries.

• We also support increased funding for export promotion through the Department of Commerce.

• We support reform of U.S. export controls on the principles proposed by Secretary Gates in March of this year.

• We support prioritizing negotiation of China's accession to the Government Procurement Agreement of the WTO, with sub-central as well as central government commitments. This would provide welcome assurance of future access to important markets for both American and Chinese companies.

• We support resumption of negotiation of a bilateral investment treaty to support both American investment in China, recognizing the large role of the state-owned sector, and Chinese investment in the U.S.

• Finally, we believe the United States must strengthen its own competitiveness by examining R&D tax credits, developing a forward-looking national energy policy, maintaining immigration rules that attract talented engineers and scientists to our country, improving our educational system, reducing the fiscal deficit to a sustainable level and similar measures. To a great extent, our fate is in our own hands and does not depend on others.

Thank you for the opportunity to appear. I look forward to your questions.

———

PREPARED STATEMENT OF THEA MEI LEE

SEPTEMBER 22, 2010

Chairman Dorgan, Co-Chairman Levin, Members of the Commission, thank you for the invitation to participate in today's important hearing on behalf of the eleven and a half million working men and women of the AFL–CIO.

Intellectual property rights enforcement is often assumed to be of interest only to business, but in fact, it is vitally important to American workers, as it impacts jobs, wages, innovation and growth, consumer safety, tax revenues, and the reputation of American products.

Other issues (including worker rights, currency manipulation, and subsidies) have often dominated labor's policy priorities with respect to China, but the lax enforcement of IPR protections remains a key contributing factor to our lopsided trade relationship. Both in the arts and entertainment sector, where copyrights are routinely ignored, and in the manufacturing sector, where counterfeit parts and products are rampant, billions of dollars in revenues and thousands of good jobs are at stake.

Moreover, taking steps now to address the Chinese government's flagrant violation of its international obligations with respect to IPR is crucial to setting a sustainable long-term trajectory for our bilateral relationship, especially with respect to technology transfer and innovation. This will impact American jobs for generations into the future.

We often hear business and government officials tout the promise of the Chinese market, and, of course, it is both large and fast-growing. But meaningful access to that market for American producers and workers is severely undercut by IPR infringement. If American entertainment products and software cannot sell at a reasonable price in the Chinese marketplace, and if the legitimate owners of those products are not able to receive their fair share of the revenues, then the "size" of the Chinese market is, for all intents and purposes, a tiny fraction of what it ought to be.

Similarly, American products are in direct competition with Chinese-produced counterfeits, costing jobs in third-country markets, as well as in the United States.

As Paul Almeida, president of the AFL–CIO Department for Professional Employees, told a Senate committee this summer, "Intellectual property equates to jobs and income for American workers. Theft of intellectual property raises unemployment and cuts income. For too many workers in the United States today, both jobs and income are hard to come by. If the United States allows attacks on intellectual property to go unanswered, it puts good livelihoods at risk."

The breadth and depth of the IPR problem in China are vast. According to a 2008 USTR report on China: "IPR infringement continued to affect products, brands, and technologies from a wide range of industries, including films, music and sound recordings, publishing, business and entertainment software, pharmaceuticals, chemicals, information technology, apparel, athletic footwear, textile fabrics and floor coverings, consumer goods, food and beverages, electrical equipment, automotive parts and industrial products, among many others."

In addition, IPR infringement means that American consumers face risk of substandard or even dangerous products in a wide range of areas. According to USTR, "China's widespread counterfeiting not only harms the business interests of foreign right holders, but also includes many products that pose a direct threat to the health and safety of consumers in the United States, China and elsewhere, such as pharmaceuticals, food and beverages, batteries, automobile parts, industrial equipment, and toys, among many other products."

In terms of the global IPR enforcement problem, China looms large, especially in terms of counterfeited and pirated products. The GAO reports that, "According to CBP data, seized counterfeit goods are dominated by products from China. During fiscal years 2004 through 2009, China accounted for about 77 percent of the aggregate value of goods seized in the United States" [GAO, "Intellectual Property: Observations on Efforts to Quantify the Economic Effects of Counterfeit and Pirated Goods," 2010].

Over many years, the U.S. government has made repeated attempts to cajole, pressure, or convince the Chinese government to improve its IPR enforcement record, through the use of Special 301 cases, priority watch lists, the Joint Committee on Commerce and Trade, and, finally, WTO cases.

While there have certainly been some improvements in China's legal framework, violations of IPR remain rampant, and the Chinese government continues to introduce new and problematic policies, including most recently the indigenous innovation policy, which sought to impose technology transfer and purchasing requirements on companies seeking to do business in China, violating China's IPR and procurement commitments.

This summer USTR filed a request for a WTO dispute panel, challenging several aspects of China's IPR law and enforcement regime. First, the request questioned quantitative thresholds in China's criminal law that must be met in order to start criminal prosecutions or obtain criminal convictions for copyright piracy and trademark counterfeiting. Second, the request contested Chinese rules for allowing IPR-infringing goods seized by Chinese customs authorities to be released into commerce following the removal of fake labels or other infringing features, contrary to WTO rules. Third, USTR challenged the denial of copyright protection for works awaiting Chinese censorship approval. Chinese copyright law provides no protection for copyright holders before censorship approval is granted.

We appreciate USTR's initiative in bringing this case to the WTO and hope that our government will continue to insist that the Chinese government fully comply with international norms in this important area.

Innovation and creativity fuel the most vibrant sectors of the U.S. economy, including the arts, entertainment and media sector and manufacturing. Both of these are enormously important to American workers, and both are hard hit by the Chinese government's failure to protect IPR.

A recent AFL–CIO Executive Council statement on piracy laid out the challenge in the arts, entertainment, and media sector: "Entertainment professionals may work for multiple employers on multiple projects and face gaps in their employment. Payment for the work they have completed helps sustain them and their families through underemployment and unemployment. For American Federation of Television and Radio Artists (AFTRA) recording artists in 2008, 90 percent of income derived from sound recordings was directly linked to royalties from physical CD sales and paid digital downloads. Screen Actors Guild (SAG) members working under the feature film and TV contract that same year derived 43 percent of their total compensation from residuals. Residuals derived from sales to secondary markets funded 65 percent of the International Alliance of Theatrical Stage Employees (IATSE) [Motion Picture Industry] Health Plan and 36 percent of the SAG Health and Pension Plan. Writers Guild of America, East (WGAE)-represented writers often depend on residual checks to pay their bills between jobs; in some cases, the residual amounts can be as much as initial compensation. Online theft robs hard-earned income and benefits from the professionals who created the works."

In the manufacturing sector, the estimates of losses from counterfeiting run to billions of dollars. Again, the victims include workers, who face lost jobs and income. From auto parts to circuit breakers, counterfeiting endangers all of us with unreliable products. It then taints the original products with the inferior quality of the counterfeits. As with the arts, entertainment, and media industries, the consequences include a diminished incentive to invest and a downward spiral for U.S. workers and our economy.

The question posed by the Commission is "Will China Protect Intellectual Property?" I believe that the answer depends on our government's actions. To date, despite many efforts, we have not done enough to insist that the Chinese government fully comply with its international obligations. Until the price for non-compliance exceeds the gains, American workers and businesses will continue to pay a high price, and the Chinese government will continue on its current short-sighted path.

———

PREPARED STATEMENT OF GREG FRAZIER

SEPTEMBER 22, 2010

Mr. Chairman, Members of the Commission:

Better access to the Chinese market lies at the heart of the American film community's strategy to protect the American jobs at risk from the attacks of Chinese film and television pirates. We cannot compete with free; Chinese film pirates are not only thieves, they are our competitors—competitors who we have subsidized.

American men and women create and produce the entertainment Chinese pirates peddle; US finances underwrite the profits Chinese pirates stash into their bank accounts. Attacking this problem, leveling this playing field, and protecting the American jobs at risk are multifaceted—better Chinese laws and more commitment to enforce those laws—but unless the market barriers are removed, those efforts will fall short.

China's filmed entertainment market is a paradox: Crippled by one of the highest piracy rates in the world—we estimated the piracy rate at over 90 percent in a recent study—the market for films for theatrical release is growing faster than most other markets. 2009 box office revenues for US companies doubled from 2008, but still only reached levels approximate to the US box office for less than one month.

This growth is not coming at the expense of the Chinese industry—American films are not threatening to crowd out the local industry—the Chinese film industry is growing rapidly as well. The number of domestic films produced in China has tripled since 2003, and box office from domestic films grew almost 50 percent from 2008.

MARKET BARRIERS = MORE PIRACY

China's film market is also one of the most restricted in the world. MPAA's[1] work to open the market is critical to growing jobs in the US industry, as well as being a key element of its content protection work in China: There is no shortage of US films in China; they are readily available in pirated form. The barriers China enforces only keep out the legitimate products and companies; the purveyors of pirated films have no regard for the rules enforced against US companies.

---

[1] The Motion Picture Association of America (MPAA) represents the six major US motion picture studios: Paramount Pictures Corporation; Sony Pictures Entertainment Inc.; The Walt Disney Studios; Twentieth Century Fox Film Corporation; Universal City Studios LLLP; and Warner Bros. Entertainment Inc.

China maintains a quota on the number of foreign films it allows into its market each year: 20. In addition, it imposes several restrictions on US businesses in the home entertainment and television business that do not exist elsewhere. Keep in mind as you review the list of barriers that these barriers affect only legitimate businesses, the businesses that play by the rules. Just as the pirates ignore intellectual property rights, they are neither bound by nor feel any obligation to abide by the restrictions affect our members:

- Foreign Investment Restrictions—China limits foreign ownership in cinemas and in video distribution companies to 49 percent. In the television sector, companies wholly or jointly owned by foreign entities are prohibited from investing in the broadcast industry.
- Television Quotas—China restricts foreign television drama and film programming to no more than 25 percent of total airtime, and other foreign programming to no more than 15 percent of total air time. Foreign programming is banned during prime time and may not constitute more than 30 percent of pay television channels. Foreign animation is restricted to no more than 40 percent of total airtime and importers of foreign animation must produce a like amount of domestic animation.
- Screen Quota—The government sets strict guidelines for foreign films. The total time for foreign films cannot exceed one-third of the total screen time.
- Import Duties—Import duties on theatrical and home video products are sometimes assessed on the potential royalty generation of an imported film, a method of assessment which is excessive and inconsistent with international practice of assessing such duties on the value of the underlying imported physical media. Excessive import duties place a severe drag on investments and impede distribution of legitimate filmed entertainment product thus increasing demand for pirate product.
- Retransmission of Foreign Satellite Signals—Local cable networks may not carry foreign satellite channels without government approval or landing permits, which currently are limited to Guangdong and a handful of foreign channels. Moreover, foreign satellite channels beaming into China are required to uplink from a government owned encrypted satellite platform. The annual fee for each channel remains excessively high at $100,000.
- Restrictions on Retailers—Foreign retailers are precluded from selling home video products without entering into a qualifying joint venture with a Chinese firm. The number of legitimate distribution points remains far less than the number of pirate distribution points.
- Blackout Periods During Peak Seasons—The government has historically decreed "black-out periods" during which no new foreign films may be released, to prevent competition with Chinese films released during the same period. Such blackouts typically occur during national holidays or coincide with political events.

None of these barriers, however, cap the Chinese audience's appetite for the filmed entertainment the American film community produces. You can get virtually any US film you want in China. You may not find it in the cinema, the local television channel, nor video store, but you can find it—in pirated form, either as a counterfeit DVD or at a Chinese website that has obtained the product illegally.

The export and transshipment of pirate optical discs from and through China continues to grow, especially pirate DVDs of US films. Transshipments flow out of China to destinations worldwide, including the US, through express mail and courier companies. The recent emergence of high-quality, counterfeit Blu-ray DVDs supplied in large volumes to businesses and consumers throughout the world over Chinese retail and auction websites is among the latest examples of China's export piracy problem.

Unfortunately, too many look at the harm of buying an illegal DVD for $2.00 in the Silk Market as victimless, perhaps even as a souvenir of a trip to Beijing. Besides morally wrong, there are at least two other things wrong about that. First, it is not a $2.00 theft. Most likely, the movie on that disc was camcorded in a theater. Illegal camcords account for roughly ninety percent of all the illegal movies in the world, and China is becoming a haven for camcorders. In the first half of this year, our research indicates that 24 camcords occurred in China. A typical MPAA member company movie may cost as much as $100 million to make. So, the person who camcorded the movie, who stole it off the screen, committed a $100 million theft.

Second, film piracy is not a victimless crime. According to a report the RAND Corporation produced in 2009, organized criminal syndicates around the world are frequently engaged in film piracy. It generates enormous profits at, unfortunately, little risk of apprehension. For example, the study identified Chinese gangs with operations as far away as the UK engaged in the trafficking illegal DVDs. It is possible the $2.00 you spend for that souvenir may not be going to an organized crime, but there is a very high likelihood it is.

WHAT TO DO?

The American film community, alone, and in cooperation with other industries and with the US government has engaged for years in a dialogue with the Chinese about amending and strengthening China's intellectual property laws.

As the market increasingly turn to the online environment, we need to make sure it is a safe market and market in which the investment of the US film community can be protected. That is the case all around the world, and including in China.

Our priority with respect to China's intellectual property laws today is urging China to address its Internet piracy problem. We believe China must provide adequate protection in the digital environment by criminalizing end-user piracy, adding reference to the exclusive rights provided in the law, criminalizing violations of the anti-circumvention provisions for technological protection measures (TPMs) and rights management information, criminalizing Internet offenses that are without profit motive but that have affect rights holders on a commercial scale, and eliminating distinctions between crimes of entities and individuals.

To foster legitimate electronic commerce, it is imperative that China establish adequate liability for ISPs for piracy related offenses and satisfactory measures for notice-and-takedown of websites offering pirate materials. Such provision will foster a responsible partnership between the content industries and the delivery networks.

The core of the problem, however, is whether the government has the will to protect the creative works American men and film produce. In your invitation to testify, you asked that I comment the various campaigns the authorities have undertaken over the years to enforce copyright violations. Some have been more successful than others. Many have simply been show campaigns, with little discernable results. Few, if any, however, have been enduring.

Let me illustrate: Across the street from the Silk Markets was a store simply named "DVD CDs." We prevailed upon the authorities to raid it not once, but three times in the course of years. I met with a senior Chinese official after the third of those and he bragged that the store had become a sporting goods and luggage retailer. After the meeting, we drove there and sure enough, through the windows I could see golf clubs and suitcases. When we entered, we were quickly ushered through a curtained passageway and into a back room with virtually any pirated DVD I could want.

Commitment. The government has a legislative framework that, while it needs some improvement, is fairly good. In addition, it has shown it can clean up the streets and stop infringement—it was impossible, for example, to find any counterfeit Olympics' goods two years ago. And, we have increasingly seen in recent months the government crack down on online content it finds objectionable—mostly pornography and political content.

But, that some commitment, that same will, has too often fallen short with respect to US filmed entertainment, to the detriment of your constituents working to produce it.

We believe we have to continue to press the Chinese for more and more effective copyright enforcement. The work you and your colleagues perform in continuing to raise this problem is invaluable. The work the Administration has performed, and continues to undertake, is as well.

That said, I do think it is time we give serious consideration to the effectiveness of some of the bilateral engagements on intellectual property rights. We do need to make a serious appraisal of the accomplishments of the Joint Committee on Commerce and Trade and its intellectual property rights working group. I cannot say today what the course is to improve it, but I can say we would be remiss if we were simply to continue business as usual.

I do know we have to improve access to the Chinese entertainment market. I will conclude where I began: The men and women in the American film community produce the most anticipated, most watched, most memorable movies in the world. In artistic and business terms, they can, and do, compete with anyone. However, they cannot stay on the job if they have to continue to compete with pirates stealing their works. We cannot compete with free.

We need to work to remove the barriers to the Chinese market—not overnight nor all at once, but to set a process by which the playing field levels. We believe that the next six months represents a unique window in that process. Last December, the World Trade Organization (WTO) ruled in favor of the complaint the US government brought against some of these key market barriers. And I want to thank, again, and commend the incredible effort the men and women of the Office of the US Trade Representative did in successfully pursuing this case.

The Chinese government has committed itself to complying with this decision by next March. We applaud them for the commitment; we await the details. We believe it is critical—to grow US jobs and to protect the movies in China—that these barriers come down in a way that sets in place a dynamism in the Chinese market that enables the US film community to grow, and that sustains the growth in the Chinese industry.

You and your colleagues meet with Chinese officials frequently. On this issue and on behalf of the Americans at work in the US film industry, if I could ask you one thing, it would be: Tell the Chinese officials how closely you are following their work to comply with the WTO ruling. Tell them how high a priority fulsome, good faith compliance is to improving the bilateral relationship. Tell them how important it is to China's place in the world, to it earning the respect of the international community, that it complies with its international obligations.

And one more thing, tell them to see a US movie, a legitimate one.

Thank you.

––––––

PREPARED STATEMENT OF RICHARD P. SUTTMEIER

SEPTEMBER 22, 2010

Mr. Chairman, Members of the Commission,

It is a pleasure to be here with you today; thank you for inviting my participation. My comments will deal mainly with China's evolving technology and industrial policies, and the role of intellectual property in them. Let me make the following points and then attempt to answer any questions you may have.

1. Concerns about intellectual property rights in China are usefully seen against the background of growing international attention to intellectual property. On one hand, countries and companies around the world are coming to see intellectual property as a key component of competitiveness; a number of national governments, including China, have introduced national IP strategies. At the same time, there is also considerable international dissatisfaction with the norms and procedures by which international IP regimes operate.[1] Growing interest in clean energy technologies in the face of worries over climate change reinforce the increasing importance of IP but also highlight some of the areas of international dissensus.[2]

2. We should recognize that there have been many changes in Chinese thinking about intellectual-property over the past two decades, including a variety of legal and institutional steps (e.g., new courts) taken to protect intellectual property. The growing number of Chinese innovators have acquired an interest in protecting IPR, and there is official recognition that China's aspirations for indigenous innovation are unlikely to be met without a far more credible intellectual property protection regime. At the same time, the production of intellectual property has also acquired a central role in Chinese thinking about their technological future and in the aggressive national technology and industrial policies now in course to realize that future. For the international community engaged with China, these changes are both encouraging and troubling. The encouragement comes from the sense that Chinese companies and the Chinese state see it in their interest to promote a more robust intellectual property protection system. The concerns come from the fact that the implementation of China's industrial policy sometimes puts the intellectual property rights of foreigners at risk.

3. In 2006, China introduced its "Medium to Long-Term Plan For Scientific and Technological Development" (MLP). The plan is a very ambitious effort to make China an "innovative society" by 2020 by encouraging the development of "indigenous innovation." The MLP puts a premium on the production of intellectual property; it expects that by the end of the plan period, the number citations to papers produced by Chinese scientists will have entered the world's top 10 countries. It also hopes to become part of the top 15 countries in terms of patents granted.

The term, "indigenous innovation" is a rather imperfect rendering of the Chinese "zizhu chuangxin," a term which defies easy translation and, as a result, has given rise to some confusion among English speakers. While "indigenous" captures part of the meaning, so might "independent," "homegrown," "self-initiated," "original"

––––––

[1] One useful review of the variety of views currently found in the international discourse on IP can be found in Scenarios for the Future, a 2008 report of the European Patent Office.

[2] Bernice Lee, Ilian Iliev, and Felix Preston. Who Owns Our Low Carbon Future? Intellectual Property in Energy Technologies. London, Chatham House.

and several other terms. In the face of confusion among foreigners and, indeed, among Chinese themselves, the Chinese Ministry of Science and Technology has suggested that *zizhu chuangxin* be understood as encompassing (1) genuinely "original innovation" (*yuanshi chuangxin*), (2) "integrated innovation" (*jicheng chuangxin*, or the fusing of existing technologies in new ways), and (3) "re-innovation" (*yinjin xiaohua xishou zaichuangxin*), which involves the assimilation and improvement of imported technologies. In desperation, some officials of the Ministry have suggested that *zizhu chuangxin* be translated simply as "innovation."

Confusion over translation, however, should not mask the deeper policy and cultural significance of the term. It grows out of China's fear of dependency on foreign technology, and what that means for the development of national security capabilities and the relative gains that China's manufacturers might realize in the global economy. In addition, the concern for "*zizhu chuangxin*" has roots in a deep cultural concern that as a great civilization, China should again become a leader in science and technology, as it once was. With these considerations in mind, the term might better be translated as "sovereign innovation."

The ambiguity surrounding the meaning of "*zizhu chuangxin*" has meant that it has been available as a symbol for the policy entrepreneurship of various groups in China's technical community (membership in which is drawn from industrial, academic, and government circles). For some, it has justified the pursuit of techno-nationalist objectives intended to build up a China-focused national innovation system. For others, it supports a more techno-globalist vision in which growing Chinese capabilities in research and development are married with global technology flows and globalized R&D to produce and innovation system that is not bounded by narrow economic nationalism. The challenge for the international community is to identify and strengthen the hands of those with the latter orientation.

The pursuit of "*zizhu chuangxin*" and the making of an "innovative society" in China by the year 2020 involves a significant expansion of R&D spending. But China has long suffered from a serious gap between R&D activities and an inability to realize commercial and other gains from turning new knowledge into practical innovations. China is attempting to overcome this gap by incentivizing Chinese industrial enterprises to take the challenges of innovation seriously. Therefore a major thrust of the MLP is to transform Chinese enterprises into centers of innovation and leaders of the national innovation system. A variety of "implementing policies" in support of the MLP are intended to privilege Chinese enterprises and support the development of Chinese intellectual property and Chinese technical standards. These policies in support of "indigenous innovation" have tended to push China in the techno-nationalist direction, in the view of many foreign observers, and have elicited widespread international concern.

The MLP contains targets for the development of products containing Chinese intellectual property as well as technical standards based on Chinese IP. As these targets have been operationalized, they have resulted in an incentive structure for Chinese companies, universities, and research institutes that rewards the filing of patents as a measure of success. It is not surprising, therefore, that there has been a steady growth in patenting over the past five years—although the quality of many of these patents has been questioned.

The elements of this incentive structure include, in the first instance, the use of IP production (measured in terms of papers and patents) for evaluating R&D projects and for awarding new R&D grants. But, in addition, IP criteria have been built into government procurement policies, and policies for technical standards. Thus, in ways that are rather unusual by international norms, China has proposed that products qualifying for government procurement should contain Chinese intellectual property. Apart from the ambiguity of what this policy might mean (what is "Chinese intellectual property"?; how is it determined?), foreign companies have been concerned that they will be excluded from an increasingly lucrative Chinese government procurement market, depending on how the policy is implemented. Although the central government appears to be backing away from the more draconian interpretations, local governments have substantial discretion in interpreting it and have been slower in adjusting policy implementation in ways that are more consistent with international norms.

While the promotion of the development of Chinese IP as part of the MLP illustrates the growing importance of strong intellectual property rights protection in Chinese thinking, new policy proposals in the area technical standards illustrate the persistence of sympathies for weaker IP. In this case, China has in recent years been troubled by what it considers to be excessive royalty fees charged for the use of certain technical standards. As a result, it has shown considerable interest in trying to forge new directions for the "patents in standards" problem, such that the

IP provisions of the Chinese standardization system would reflect what Chinese officials believe to be a "fairer" formula for royalty payments.

4. There is no simple way to respond to China's "indigenous innovation" initiatives, especially when they are understood in terms of "sovereign innovation." Nevertheless, responses along several tracks are appropriate. First, China should be pushed to honor its commitment to join the Government Procurement Agreement sooner rather than later. Second, the United States should build on its extensive science and technology contacts with China via commercial, academic, and government channels to promote a vision of innovation that transcends a limited and narrow techno-nationalism. A case can be made that some of China's policies in support of "indigenous innovation" actually work against the achievement of the "innovative society" goal, and this case should be made frequently and forcefully in contacts with Chinese policymakers and members of the technical community.

Policies with regard to procurement and standards have led to the bureaucratization of IP issues, and the complexities of central government-local government relations in the implementation of policies have made things worse. As in other areas of Chinese public policy, policymaking and policy implementation are not as coherent as a "China Inc." image might lead us to believe. It is unfortunate that the areas of incoherence can, and often do, impose costs on China's foreign commercial partners. A positive interpretation of these problems is that China is in a phase of development that makes incoherence inescapable, but is trending in the direction of greater coherence and, hence, a future with fewer conflicts over IP matters. A more troubling interpretation, though, is that China is on a trajectory which will be characterized both by greater policy coherence and policy development in the areas of IP and standards which will be more difficult to harmonize with international norms.

What is less subject to interpretation, though, is that China is seriously and understandably committed to its own scientific and technological development and innovative capacity, and there is little that the international community can do to change this. Instead, members of the international community have to devise ways of exploiting that development by encouraging its further internationalization, monitoring its progress, and preparing for strategic interventions to take advantage of the new opportunities it will offer.

5. In joining WTO, China has pledged that technology transfer requirements would not be a condition for foreign investment. That we continue to hear complaints about coerced transfers indicates that China is either ignoring its WTO commitments or has found new policy tools to induce transfers.

In many industries, though, including clean energy, the Chinese market is so attractive to international companies that the wresting of some degree of technology transfer from investments is unavoidable. In raising this point, we are reminded that technology transfer, more often than not, is a business decision. We should also be reminded that, except in rare cases, the business value of intellectual property depends not solely on the quality of the intellectual contribution embodied in the IP, but also on the "complementary assets" which make it possible to exploit the value of the intellectual property.

In the area of clean energy technologies, we are increasingly seeing that China is providing those complementary assets at a rate, and on a scale, that makes it a magnet for owners of IP to conduct business there. There have been a number of recent reports to this effect; I would call your attention to a most recent one issued by Agence France Presse, entitled "China a Beacon for Foreign Clean Tech Firms."[3] According to this account, China has surpassed United States this year as the most attractive market for investments in renewable energy technologies, in large part because it has become ". . .a very good market to commercialize technology at scale. . . ." Furthermore, China is providing the financial resources to facilitate the transformation of important technical ideas into commercial products. Quoting Nicholas Parker of the US-based Cleantech Group, "Things are tough for companies here (in the West). . . .we have a shortage of debt financing. The money for deployment, for building wind farms or for building a factory where you tend to use debt financing, has dried up due to the crisis on Wall Street. That shortage doesn't exist in China." Add to China's advantages the fact that it is creating an increasingly competent R&D system with a growing number of capable scientists and engineers. In short, China offers markets, financing, R&D capabilities, and a supportive policy environment for clean energy; it is not surprising that owners of intellectual property will risk IPR infringements by taking their business there.

6. The points made above are intended to suggest that US thinking about intellectual property rights in China needs a fairly major overhaul. That there are IPR

---

[3] http://www.abs-cbnnews.com/business/09/19/10/china-beacon-foreign-clean-tech-firms

abuses in China is beyond doubt; they affect Chinese innovators as well as for-eigners, and should be opposed. But it is also clear that the value of intellectual property is not solely intrinsic to the ideas themselves, but requires an environment rich in complementary assets for that value to be released. It is becoming increas-ingly clear that in the area of clean energy, policy failures resulting from what appears to be a broken political system in United States are leading to the squan-dering of the complementary assets we once had in abundance.

The globalization of innovation puts a premium on both the ability to produce in-tellectual property, but also to exploit it. The global innovation system is usefully thought of as a complex network of interconnected nodes. The United States has been a "supernode" in this network for the last 60 years as the center of IP creation and IP exploitation and, importantly, a magnet for innovators from around the world. Many signs indicate that China is becoming a new "supernode" in spite of the difficulties of its IPR regime. While it is important for the United States to con-tinue to work with China in moving that regime towards international norms, there clearly is a need for new thinking about intellectual property in China, and for a far more imaginative approach to engaging China on these issues.

———

PREPARED STATEMENT OF HON. SANDER LEVIN, A U.S. REPRESENTATIVE FROM MICHIGAN, COCHAIRMAN CONGRESSIONAL-EXECUTIVE COMMISSION ON CHINA

SEPTEMBER 22, 2010

The topic of today's hearing is of the utmost importance to American workers and American business. American workers and businesses lose billions of dollars each year to Chinese intellectual property rights infringement.

The Chinese government has failed to comply with the commitments to protect intellectual property rights that it made as a member of the WTO, and it continues to undermine protections for intellectual property contained in its own laws and reg-ulations. By shining a spotlight on how China's flagrant abuse of international rules governing intellectual property rights undermines the rule of law, this Commission has an important role to play.

The headline of a recent and detailed Wall Street Journal article says it all: "China Spooks Auto Makers: Foreign Companies Fear New Rules on Electric Cars Will Erode Intellectual Property." The article notes that "China's government is con-sidering plans that could force foreign automakers to hand over cutting-edge elec-tric-vehicle technology to Chinese companies in exchange for access to the nation's huge market." The article goes on to say that China's Ministry of Industry and In-formation Technology is preparing a 10-year plan "that could compel foreign auto-makers that want to produce electric vehicles in China to share critical technologies by requiring the companies to enter joint ventures in which they are limited to a minority stake." The article notes how Beijing's program of so-called "indigenous in-novation" discriminates against foreign companies, and is said to be "aimed at gain-ing control of foreign intellectual property."

China's industrial policies have a common thread: they have the purpose or the effect of tilting the playing field to favor Chinese companies and against U.S. com-panies and workers. That is not a sound or sustainable basis for a mutually bene-ficial U.S.-China relationship. Nor is it a viable foundation for the development of the rule of law in China.

There is an ever widening chasm between what we hear from the Chinese govern-ment about the protection of intellectual property in China, and what we know to be true about the protection of intellectual property in China.

We hear that the legal infrastructure supporting intellectual property rights has improved; we hear that courts are becoming more professionalized and skilled at handling complex issues related to intellectual property; we hear that Chinese rights holders are turning to Chinese courts to assert their rights more than in the past, and that there has been a measurable increase in the number of civil intellec-tual property cases in Chinese courts; we hear that foreign plaintiffs are winning intellectual property cases at increasing rates.

That is what we hear. But this is what we know:

We know that the American Chamber of Commerce in China surveyed its mem-bers this year and found that 63 percent rated intellectual property rights enforce-ment in China as "ineffective." We know that intellectual property infringement in China is more widespread than before, and that counterfeit exports have increased; we know that enforcement of intellectual property judgments is difficult in China, that damages are still inadequate by international standards, and that the Chinese government has not taken sufficient steps to address difficulties in the gathering of evidence; we know that high value and volume thresholds must be met in order to initiate criminal prosecution of intellectual property infringement, that administrative fines are too low and civil damages too inadequate and imposed too infrequently to serve as deterrents, and that infringers view them merely as a cost of doing business.

In sum, we know that the Chinese government could be doing far more to protect intellectual property rights, but it is not doing so.

We know that in 2009, 79 percent of intellectual property-infringing product seizures at the U.S. border were of Chinese origin; we know that China's State-Owned Assets Supervision and Administration Commission has the power to require Chinese state-owned enterprises to certify that all software they use is properly licensed, but that it has not required state-owned enterprises to provide such certification; we know that production of counterfeit auto parts experienced a period of significant growth in China in recent years, and that a significant portion of counterfeit auto parts in China are manufactured in areas the Chinese government has designated as auto parts export zones.

We know that the Chinese government's market access barriers lead consumers to the black market. We know, for example, that to enforce its policies of censorship, the Chinese government limits the number of foreign films, books, and other media that may be distributed legally in China. We know that these limits effectively create markets for pirates. It is bad enough that Chinese government censorship practices violate international human rights standards. But let me state this clearly: Chinese government censorship leads consumers to the black market, and that, in turn, incentivizes the violation of intellectual property rights. The Chinese government often denies the link between human rights and the commercial rule of law. But the link is clear, and the Chinese government itself creates this link. Chinese government censorship leads to the violation of intellectual property rights.

There can be no doubt that China's flagrant abuse of international rules undermines the rule of law. There is no doubt that widespread intellectual property rights infringement in China continues to affect products, brands, and technologies from a wide range of industries, and imperils the health and safety of both American and Chinese consumers, and imposes billions of dollars of losses yearly on American businesses and workers.

Change is necessary—both in the Chinese government's behavior, and in the action we take in response. I look forward to our witnesses' testimony.

———

PREPARED STATEMENT OF HON. CHRISTOPHER SMITH, A U.S. REPRESENTATIVE FROM NEW JERSEY, RANKING MEMBER, CONGRESSIONAL-EXECUTIVE COMMISSION ON CHINA

SEPTEMBER 22, 2010

Thank you, Mr. Chairman, and welcome to everyone this afternoon.

Mr. Chairman, the Global Intellectual Property Center estimates annual U.S. losses caused by intellectual property infringement of almost $125 billion in the automotive, recording, pharmaceutical, and software industry industries alone, and we know that the Chinese government is the cause of most of the problem.

China tolerates—in some cases, probably, encourages—widespread infringement of American intellectual property rights, and then exports U.S.-property rights infringing products right back to us. According to the U.S. Trade Representative's 2010 "Special 301 Report," 79 percent of infringing products seized at our border were of Chinese origin. I wonder how many jobs that translates into—how many American jobs would return if key foreign countries enforced the intellectual property agreements they signed?

I hope our witnesses address this question, as well as discuss the tools the executive branch has to take truly decisive action to protect American intellectual property—our workers and our economy. In the Trade Act of 1974, Congress provided the executive with all the authority it needs to remedy many trade injustices—injustices to our own workers as well as to foreign workers exploited in sweatshops. The executive branch has rarely made use of these—in fact, in 2006 then-Congressman Ben Cardin and I joined the AFL–CIO in a Section 301 petition to President Bush, which was denied, and I recently urged AFL–CIO leaders to petition President Obama under Section 301 of the Trade Act. In that petition the issue was the denial of the basic worker rights in China, and its adverse effect on American workers, and Section 301 provided WTO-consistent remedies. So we have two very serious issues here—the harm done to U.S. workers, and the exploitation of Chinese workers.

Mr. Chairman, our government has a responsibility to take action here. The unemployment rate was just reported as 9.6 percent in my state, New Jersey, and in fact is 9.6 percent nationally—and this means millions of people struggling to make house payments, to feed their families. We need to ensure the President and the USTR are using all the tools they have to fix the problem.

———

PREPARED STATEMENT OF HON. CARL LEVIN, A U.S. SENATOR FROM MICHIGAN, MEMBER, CONGRESSIONAL-EXECUTIVE COMMISSION ON CHINA

SEPTEMBER 22, 2010

I commend the Chairman and Cochairman of the CECC for holding this important hearing. Despite nearly 10 years as a member of the WTO, China continues to engage in unfair trade practices. Two areas of concern I would like the Commission to look at are the actions China is taking to favor its domestic renewable energy technology sector and automotive parts counterfeiting.

We should all be alarmed by China's attempts to dominate the renewable energy industry through measures that discriminate against foreign manufacturers. China does this by requiring the use of domestic suppliers and production for green and renewable technology. This was validated in USTR's 2009 Special 301 report on China which noted U.S. industry concerns about the possibility that Chinese laws or policies in a variety of fields might be used to unfairly favor domestic intellectual property over foreign intellectual property. The report stated the concerns are, "especially acute in light of Chinese Government policies that appear to establish a procurement preference for domestically innovated products." China also requires a significant percentage of these products be exported, in order to guarantee that its domestic companies will dominate this important sector.

China is trying to have it both ways: protecting its home market while exporting most of its production. The New York Times reported that China protects its domestic producers by requiring that 80 percent of the equipment used in Chinese solar power plants be made in China. At the same time, over 95 percent of China's solar panel production is exported to the United States and Europe.

China also has designs to dominate clean car technology. According to the Wall Street Journal, China is preparing a 10-year plan to turn China into the world's leader in developing and producing battery-powered cars and hybrids. The draft plan suggests that China could compel foreign auto makers who want to produce electric vehicles in China to transfer critical technology by requiring those companies to enter into joint ventures where the foreign auto maker would be limited to a minority stake. I agree with the foreign auto executive that said it is, "tantamount to China strong-arming foreign auto makers to give up battery, electric-motor, and control technology in exchange for market access." With such government mandated policies in place, once all of the technology is transferred the Chinese joint venture partner will become a competitor.

At a time when American manufacturers are working hard to compete in the emerging field of green technologies, China must not be allowed to unfairly or illegally undermine those efforts. The United Steel Workers of America has filed a trade petition accusing China of violating the WTO by subsidizing exports of clean energy equipment. I have urged the administration to investigate these allegations.

I am also concerned about the counterfeiting of auto parts, concerns that extend beyond monetary losses to U.S. firms and directly impact human health and safety. A counterfeit auto part could be the wheel or the brakes on your car. Since counterfeit parts are often substandard and produced with inferior materials, they put lives at risk. The Motor & Equipment Manufacturers Association (MEMA) recently testified that most counterfeits appear to be made in China.

The Gates Corporation, headquartered in Denver, CO, with operations in Michigan, is a major manufacturer of a range of belts used in motor vehicles and has faced a number of cases of counterfeit belts worldwide. When Gates tested pirated timing belts it found they were inferior to the genuine part with a significantly shorter lifespan. A counterfeit timing belt may wear and fail prematurely with serious cost, health, and safety consequences. A consumer advocacy group in China relying on Chinese media reports estimates that 70 percent of aftermarket auto parts in China are counterfeit and that approximately 13 percent of car accidents are due to fake auto parts.

In addition to the safety issues, American companies' investments in innovation and technology development are at risk. The auto parts industry's losses due to counterfeiting are enormous. MEMA conservatively estimates that counterfeit goods cost motor vehicle suppliers up to $12 billion globally in lost sales every year. Market researchers Frost and Sullivan estimated in 2006 that the global losses to motor vehicle suppliers due to counterfeiting would be as high as $45 billion in 2011. In

2007 Ford Motor Co. stated that counterfeit auto parts cost it nearly $1 billion a year. We cannot continue to allow these types of American investments and innovations to be stolen by foreign competitors.

For almost 20 years the United States has been aggressively pressing China through Section 301 trade cases to improve its intellectual property protection regime. Yet China continues to be the number one source country for counterfeit and pirated goods seized in fiscal year 2009, accounting for 79 percent or $204.7 million of the total value seized. The USTR's 2010 Special 301 report continued to list China on the Priority Watch List and stated that China continued to be a major focus of U.S. concerns. Even though China made some progress in improving its enforcement regime, the USTR said piracy rates remained at "unacceptable levels." The Chinese Government itself estimates that counterfeits constitute between 15 percent and 20 percent of all products made in China and are equivalent to about 8 percent of China's annual gross domestic product.

China's trade distorting practices need to be aggressively investigated by the USTR as we work to hold China to its WTO commitments in international trade.

SUBMISSIONS FOR THE RECORD

PREPARED STATEMENT OF ROBERT W. HOLLEYMAN, II, PRESIDENT AND CEO, BUSINESS SOFTWARE ALLIANCE

SEPTEMBER 22, 2010

We applaud the Commission for holding this very important hearing on IP protection in China. This is a critical issue for BSA and our members.

BSA is an association of the world's leading software companies and their hardware partners around the world.[1] BSA members create approximately 90 percent of the office productivity software in use in the United States and around the world.

The software industry has proven to be a remarkable engine for jobs and economic growth. The software and related services sector employed almost 2 million people in the United States in 2007 in jobs that paid 195 percent of the national average wage. This sector contributed more than $261 billion to US GDP in 2007, making it the largest of the US copyright industries.

The packaged software industry's overseas earnings contributed a $37 billion surplus to our nation's balance of trade in 2009. As much as 60 percent of revenues for the leading US software companies are generated from sales outside US borders.

A few months ago the Chief Executive Officers of twelve BSA member companies came to Washington, DC to meet with Congressional leaders and the President's senior economic team. Their message was simple—the US software industry is key to the US economy and China is a critical market for our future growth.

Two Chinese practices stand in the way of American software companies' ability to compete in China: massive illegal use of software (nearly 4 out of every 5 computer programs installed on personal computers (PCs) in China last year were being used illegally) and the development of "indigenous innovation" policies that limit our access to a broad swath of the Chinese market.

The indigenous innovation issue has received high-level attention from the US government over the past year and BSA applauds this. Progress, however, has been slow in getting China to rethink and suspend its problematic indigenous innovation policies—from government procurement, to standard-setting, to certification requirements—that pose significant market access restrictions for US software and other technology companies. These policies are characterized by significant preferences for domestic firms and requirements seeking to compel transfers of technology as a precondition for market access. More action is needed.

Given its broad-based impact on the US economy, we believe the pervasive use of illegal software in China needs intensified attention from the US government as well.

It is now an established fact that software and computers have changed the world in which we live. Information technology has made us more efficient, more productive and more creative. Software and computers deliver results on national priorities such as health care, energy, infrastructure, education, and e-government.

Software has been at the heart of this technology revolution. It is also a big part of the US industrial base, whether it is the software used by steel companies, the autos we drive, or the energy saving appliances we use in our daily lives. Software drives productivity and innovation in almost every economic sector, helping businesses of all sizes perform better in good times and bad.

We believe our country's ability to create jobs depends in large part on our ability to export. We support the President's ambitious National Export Initiative (NEI) goal of doubling US exports of goods and services over five years. We stand ready to do our part, but cannot do so if a market as critical as China is out of reach because of high levels of software piracy.

---

[1] The Business Software Alliance (www.bsa.org) is the world's foremost advocate for the software industry, working in 80 countries to expand software markets and create conditions for innovation and growth. Governments and industry partners look to BSA for thoughtful approaches to key policy and legal issues, recognizing that software plays a critical role in driving economic and social progress in all nations. BSA's member companies invest billions of dollars a year in local economies, good jobs, and next-generation solutions that will help people around the world be more productive, connected, and secure. BSA members include Adobe, Altium, Apple, Autodesk, AVEVA, AVG, Bentley Systems, CA Technologies, Cadence, Cisco Systems, CNC/Mastercam, Corel, Dassault Systèmes SolidWorks Corporation, Dell, HP, IBM, Intel, Intuit, Kaspersky Lab, McAfee, Microsoft, Minitab, PTC, Progress Software, Quark, Quest Software, Rosetta Stone, Siemens, Sybase, Symantec, Synopsys, and The MathWorks.

Here are the facts. Our annual Global Software Piracy Study undertaken by market research firm IDC estimates that nearly 4 out of every 5 software programs installed on PCs in China widely used in the government, enterprises and by consumers in 2009 were unlicensed. The Study conservatively estimates that the commercial value of those programs is $7.6 billion. That is double what it was just 4 years ago. In stark contrast, the estimated revenues from sales of PC software from US producers in China were around $1 billion.

But these numbers, large as they are, understate the problem.

Nearly as many PCs were sold to businesses in China in 2009 as to those in the United States. Our country's total exports to China in 2009 were $70 billion. If Chinese enterprises were to actually pay for just the PC software they use, we conservatively estimate that total US exports to China could grow by at least 5 percent. The impact would be higher when the broader universe of packaged software is considered. This gives you a good picture of what is at stake.

The economic harm due to the illegal use of software in China has broader consequences here at home for US jobs. Products made in China by enterprises that use illegal software hurt American competitiveness and in many cases displace US jobs. Our companies pay for their critical inputs of production, such as software, while many of their Chinese competitors do not. Chinese products made with illegal software enter our markets and undercut our goods and services. In practical terms this harms US jobs.

We need to think of the problem of illegal use of software in a different way. The problem is more pervasive, more complex, and more pernicious than it was just a few years ago. Quite frankly, the term "piracy" is outdated. It does not even begin to capture the breadth of the problem.

So what should we do?

We believe the United States should develop a comprehensive results-based trade policy with China in place of the one-off, issue-by-issue approach that guides the current relationship. Our primary measure of success should be increased US exports of goods and services.

At a recent Senate Finance Committee hearing, responding to a Senator's comment that US-China economic policy was too focused on "soothing words," Treasury Secretary Geithner said "[t]he test of these things is not what people say and it's not how many meetings you have. The test is what actually happens to the terms and conditions that US companies compete on."

We agree wholeheartedly.

For over 20 years, the United States has engaged China in round after round of discussions aimed at one-off issue resolution at periodic ministerial meetings, including improved protections for software and other forms of intellectual property. These efforts have resulted in some positive changes, but not enough. Meaningful results for our sector, as measured by increased exports of goods and services, have been lacking.

As a key element of developing and implementing a result-based trade policy, we should hold China accountable for its commitments to combat software piracy. For example, in 2004, as part of the bilateral US-China Joint Commission on Commerce and Trade (JCCT) negotiations, China committed that government entities would only use legal software. The United States has an Executive Order that requires this. Soon after this commitment was made, the Chinese government self-declared that it had fulfilled this promise, though provided no means for verification. The Chinese government also committed in the JCCT that state-owned enterprises (SOEs) would use only legal software and later made assertions that this had generally been accomplished.

Since these commitments were made, software sales by US-based companies have hardly budged while illegal use of PC software in China as a whole has doubled to $7.6 billion. At present, SOEs and other Chinese enterprises regularly use unlicensed software to operate their businesses, safe in the knowledge that there are no consequences.

Our overall goal should be increased exports of goods and services, but there are some immediate steps that we think should be taken.

The US government should press the Chinese government to:

- Devote resources to enforcement against software piracy that are commensurate with the scope of the problem.
- Cooperate with industry's efforts to bring civil cases to enforce software license compliance, including cases against SOEs.
- Implement verification and audit systems to measure performance in fulfilling commitments on government and enterprise legalization.
- Make software piracy by enterprises subject to criminal penalties.

The United States should also undertake a full examination of available trade policy remedies to address these concerns. This would include assessing whether actions can be brought under the World Trade Organization (WTO) and whether China's practices are a form of unfair competition that can be addressed by US trade laws.

The challenges that we face due to software piracy are now being compounded by Chinese policies that restrict our access to the Chinese market. Over the past several years, the Chinese government has issued a series of "indigenous innovation" policies that erect barriers to US software and other products in a quest to promote domestic champions. These Chinese policies discriminate against foreign firms through a web of preferences for Chinese-developed technology and standards and compel American and other foreign companies to relocate their R&D to China or lose the ability to sell there.

To counteract the harm caused by these policies, the US government must press the Chinese government to suspend current policies that create market access barriers and compel IP transfers, and engage in a meaningful dialogue on non-discriminatory approaches to promote innovation.

We accept that we have to do our part to help ourselves. We are doing several things. Our members continue to invest on average more than 7 percent of revenues in R&D, with some investing close to 20 percent. We are determined to improve on our already world leading software products. This investment will enable us to innovate, compete and create jobs in the United States. In China, we have had a long-standing program to pursue enforcement actions against enterprises that illegally use our software and to educate users about the importance of using legal software. To date, these efforts have produced limited results. We are committed to retooling and upgrading those enforcement and education efforts and are now in the midst of implementing a new enforcement plan in China.

SOFTWARE PIRACY IN THE CHINESE MARKET

The current rate of illegal software use in China is staggering. Recent estimates from the market research firm IDC indicate that nearly 4 out of every 5 copies (79 percent) of PC software installed in China in 2009 were illegal, with a total commercial value of $7.6 billion. These are industry averages, and understate the dire situation that piracy creates for many of our companies.

A leading source of these losses is what we describe as "end-user piracy"—the unlicensed use of software by Chinese businesses and other enterprises. Chinese authorities do not view the unlicensed use of software by enterprises as a crime. As a result, US software companies must rely on China's civil and administrative systems to pursue these infringers. The vast scale of the problem, the generally modest civil and administrative remedies available, and the time and expense of pursuing actions against individual companies mean that, in practice, the software industry is largely powerless to deter, let alone stop, the widespread illegal use of its products in China.

End-user piracy is not limited to so-called private enterprises engaged in commercial activity in China. Far from it. Unauthorized use of software is also extremely widespread in government agencies and in China's massive SOEs and the companies they own. China has repeatedly committed in the JCCT that all government agencies—including provincial and local government authorities—and SOEs would use only licensed software. US industry has seen little progress on these commitments.

Other forms of illegal software use are also prevalent. For example, hard-disk loading of software—where PC manufacturers and resellers install unlicensed software onto PCs before their sale—is widespread. After years of effort by the software industry and considerable pressure from the US government, China issued a Decree in 2006 stating that all PCs produced in or imported into China must have legal operating system software pre-installed. While implementation of this Decree resulted in a modest increase in software sales in the first year, progress since that time has been minimal, hindered largely by the government's unwillingness to verify that China's PC makers are complying with the Decree.

Physical goods piracy—including manufacture and sale of pirate CD–ROMs, each containing thousands of dollars worth of illegal business software, and counterfeiting of a virtually unlimited range of computer hardware and devices—also proceeds largely unhindered. And Internet piracy flourishes in China. China's Internet population is now by far the largest in the world, estimated at 384 million users—a figure greater than the entire US population. The Chinese government has not effectively acted to stop Internet users and website operators from distributing unlicensed software within and outside the Chinese market.

THE IMPACT ON US JOBS

While this illegal software use takes place thousands of miles from US shores, its impact is felt right here at home, in cities and towns across America.

By refusing to pay for the software they use, Chinese businesses artificially reduce their expenses and gain a competitive advantage over US firms. This enables Chinese companies to develop and manufacture products more cheaply than their US competitors.

In short, the illegal use of software by Chinese companies not only deprives US software firms of sales and revenues, but allows these Chinese companies to undercut the sales of goods and services by their US competitors, reducing the revenues of US companies, and depriving US workers of good jobs.

The US International Trade Commission is currently undertaking an investigation to better understand the scope of intellectual property infringement and China's indigenous innovation policies and the implications for US competitiveness and jobs. We are taking advantage of the opportunity to participate in this investigation and believe that the results, particularly the new economic models that may result from this work, should provide valuable information for policymakers.

A RESULTS-BASED TRADE POLICY

US industry, with the strong support of the US government, has long pressed China to protect intellectual property rights. In response, China has taken steps to improve its IP regime, such as modifications to its copyright and trademark laws, and the adoption of a regulation aimed at Internet piracy. More generally, as part of its WTO accession, China committed to following the rules-based trading system and providing adequate intellectual property protection.

But gaps remain, and enforcement of the laws is inadequate. The result is that US industry losses due to software piracy continue to grow.

Indeed, the list of needed actions by the Chinese government identified in the US Trade Representative's "Special 301" process earlier this year is extensive. The list includes enforcement-related improvements, legislative changes and market access issues. Specifically, increases in the number of criminal prosecutions and administrative actions against copyright infringers, greater resources for, and training of, IP enforcement authorities, the assignment of judges with IP expertise to hear criminal cases, and amendments to a number of laws including the copyright law, the criminal law, and the regulations that govern Internet enforcement.

Historically, industry and the US government have measured China's progress towards improved intellectual property protection based on whether China adopted these or other specific legislative and enforcement-related measures and on commitments made by the Chinese government as part of the Strategic & Economic Dialogue (S&ED), JCCT and other bilateral negotiations. It is abundantly clear, however, that this approach is not working as all of us had expected. The Chinese government has not fulfilled many key commitments and has clearly not undertaken the more sweeping steps necessary to meaningfully reduce intellectual property theft.

In the next 12–18 months, the market for PCs sold to businesses in China is expected to become the largest in the world, and yet the outlook for software sales is dismal. On this, the past does not offer grounds for optimism. The rate of PC software piracy in China has declined only 7 percentage points since 2005—from 86 to 79 percent in five years. At this rate, it will take over 40 years for China's piracy rate to come anywhere close to the level in the United States (20 percent).

We urge the US government to consider moving away from measuring progress based on whether or not China amends a specific law or undertakes a discrete commitment. Instead, we need to move to a system that measures the actual results of China's actions in terms of increased exports of US software and reductions in software piracy in the Chinese market.

Such a results-based trade policy would align well with President Obama's National Export Initiative. The President set a goal of doubling US exports in the next five years, an increase that the Administration projects will create over two million new US jobs. Increased exports of goods and services will also help to drive US economic growth more broadly; growing US exports contributed nearly 2 percentage points to US economic expansion in the last six months of 2009 alone.

This same results-based approach should be applied to China. The immediate goal should be to increase US software exports to China by 50 percent over the next two years. Given the extremely high levels of software piracy in China, this benchmark would be reasonable to achieve through a decrease in the software piracy rate. Utilizing clearly defined, concrete and measurable benchmarks to assess progress would help the United States evaluate the US-China trade relationship more accurately and encourage China to take meaningful steps to reduce illegal software use across the Chinese economy.

CHINA MUST ABIDE BY ITS TRADE OBLIGATIONS

In parallel with the use of increased exports as the measure for progress, it is necessary to ensure that China takes seriously its international obligations and other commitments.

The Chinese government appears to have taken the view that it can turn a blind eye to widespread illegal software use with no fear of violating its obligations as a member of the WTO—and with no fear of sanctions for its actions.

The US government needs trade tools to challenge Chinese practices that have the effect of depriving the United States of benefits that it legitimately expects from China's membership in the WTO. Chief among these, in our view, is China's need to make meaningful progress in reducing illegal software use and increasing market opportunities for US software suppliers.

A WTO remedy that merits consideration is that of a non-violation "nullification or impairment" claim, under Article XXIII of the General Agreement on Tariffs and Trade. Such actions are appropriate where a WTO member's conduct, while not violating the letter of the agreement, nonetheless denies or impairs a benefit accruing to another party under the WTO.

Moreover, as discussed above, the high-levels of software piracy in China also provide an unfair competitive disadvantage for Chinese firms that use unlicensed software to produce goods and run their operations in competition with US firms. We would suggest that this practice may be a form of unfair competition subject to action under US trade laws.

CONCLUSION

My testimony here demonstrates the stark reality that BSA members are facing in China.

As US Trade Representative Kirk recently remarked, "[i]ntellectual property theft in overseas markets is an export killer for American businesses and a job killer for American workers here at home." While we believe that the United States must continue to pursue a strong economic relationship with China, China's persistent failure to protect the intellectual property of US products and innovations and its discriminatory "indigenous innovation" policies seriously undermine this relationship. More importantly, China's actions are costing US jobs.

We urge the members of the Commission to explore new solutions to address this challenge—including results-based trade policies and application of new trade remedies—in order to better protect US innovators, US industry and US workers. We stand ready to assist the Commission in this endeavor. Thank you.

––––––––––

PIRACY IS A DANGER TO ENTERTAINMENT PROFESSIONALS

Submitted by the Department for Professional Employees, AFL–CIO (DPE) for the Arts, Entertainment and Media Industries Unions Affiliated with DPE

AFL–CIO EXECUTIVE COUNCIL STATEMENT, ORLANDO, FLORIDA MARCH 2, 2010

Motion pictures, television, sound recordings and other entertainment are a vibrant part of the U.S. economy. They yield one of its few remaining trade surpluses. The online theft of copyrighted works and the sale of illegal CDs and DVDs threaten the vitality of U.S. entertainment and thus its working people.

The equation is simple and ominous. Piracy costs the U.S. entertainment industry billions of dollars in revenue each year. That loss of revenue hits directly at bottom-line profits. When profits are diminished, the incentive to invest in new films, television programs, sound recordings and other entertainment drops. With less investment in future works comes less industry activity that directly benefits workers: fewer jobs, less compensation for entertainment professionals and a reduction in health and pension benefits.

Combating online theft and the sale of illegal CDs and DVDs is nothing short of defending U.S. jobs and benefits. In the case of music, experts estimate that the digital theft of sound recordings costs the U.S. economy $12.5 billion in total output and costs U.S. workers 71,060 jobs.[1] In the motion picture industry, piracy results

––––––––––

[1] Siwek, Stephen. (8/21/07). The True Cost of Sound Recording Piracy to the U.S. Economy. Retrieved from: http://www.ipi.org/IPI/IPIPublications.nsf/PublicationLookupFullText/ 5C2EE3D2107 A4C228625733E0053A1F4

in an estimated $5.5 billion in lost wages annually, and the loss of an estimated 141,030 jobs that would otherwise have been created.[2]

Illegal CDs and DVDs have afflicted even live theatre. Websites sell illegal DVDs of Broadway shows, which reduces sales of tickets and authorized CDs and DVDs. Selling illegal CDs or DVDs of plays, musicals and other shows not only steals the work of the entertainment professionals, but makes quality control impossible.

Most of the revenue that supports entertainment professionals' jobs and benefits comes from the sale of entertainment works including sales in secondary markets— that is, DVD and CD sales, legitimate downloads, royalties and, in the case of TV shows or films, repeated airings on free cable or premium pay television. Roughly 75 percent of a motion picture's revenues comes after the initial theatrical release, and more than 50 percent of scripted television production revenues are generated after the first run.

In most work arrangements, a worker receives payment for his or her effort at the completion of a project or at set intervals. The entertainment industry, however, operates on a longstanding unique business model in which compensation to workers—pay and benefit contributions—comes in two stages. Film, television and recording artists, as well as film and television writers, receive an initial payment for their work and then residuals or royalties for its subsequent use. Those payments also generate funds for their health and pension plans. The below-the-line workers, the craft and technical people who manage equipment, props, costumes, makeup, special effects and other elements of a production, also receive compensation for their work, while payment for subsequent use goes directly into their health and pension plans.

Motion picture production is a prime example. The professionals involved with the initial production of a film—the actors who perform, the craftspeople behind the scenes, the musicians who create the soundtrack and the writers who craft the story—each receive an initial payment for their work. When that work is resold in the form of DVDs or CDs, or to cable networks or to airlines or in foreign sales, a portion of these "downstream revenues" are direct compensation to the film talent or recording artists who were involved in those productions or recordings.

These residuals help keep entertainment professionals afloat between projects. Entertainment professionals may work for multiple employers on multiple projects and face gaps in their employment. Payment for the work they have completed helps sustain them and their families through underemployment and unemployment. For AFTRA recording artists in 2008, 90 percent of income derived from sound recordings was directly linked to royalties from physical CD sales and paid digital downloads. SAG members working under the feature film and TV contract that same year derived 43 percent of their total compensation from residuals. Residuals derived from sales to secondary markets funded 65 percent of the IATSE MPI Health Plan and 36 percent of the SAG Health and Pension Plan. WGAE-represented writers often depend on residual checks to pay their bills between jobs; in some cases, the residual amounts can be as much as initial compensation. Online theft robs hard-earned income and benefits from the professionals who created the works.

There are tools that can be used to fight digital piracy. Internet service providers (ISPs) have the ability to find illegal content and remove or limit access to it. To be truly effective, these sanctions must depart from the costly and ineffective legal remedies traditionally employed to counter theft of copyrighted material. The European Union is developing and implementing model policies for which the trade union movement is providing strong and critical support. These policies illustrate that there are answers that make sense in a digital age.

At the core of any effort to combat digital theft is reasonable network management, which should allow ISPs to use available tools to detect and prevent the illegal downloading of copyrighted works. With respect to lawfully distributed content, ISPs should not be allowed to block or degrade service so that both consumers and copyright would be protected.

The unions of the AFL–CIO that represent professionals in the Arts, Entertainment and Media Industries (AEMI) include Actors' Equity Association (AEA), the American Federation of Musicians (AFM), the American Federation of Television and Radio Artists (AFTRA), the American Guild of Musical Artists (AGMA), the International Alliance of Theatrical Stage Employees, Moving Picture Technicians, Artists and Allied Crafts (IATSE), the International Brotherhood of Electrical Workers (IBEW), the Office and Professional Employees International Union (OPEIU),

---

[2] Siwek, Stephen. (9/20/06). The True Cost of Sound Recording Piracy to the U.S. Economy. Retrieved from: http://www.ipi.org/IPI/IPIPublications.nsf/PublicationLookupFullText/E274F77 ADF58BD08862571F8001BA6BF

the Screen Actors Guild (SAG) and the Writers Guild of America, East (WGAE). The AEMI unions are wholly in support of the widest possible access to content on the Internet and the principles of net neutrality, so long as intellectual property rights—and the hundreds of thousands of jobs that are at stake—are respected.

Some would like to portray the debate over Internet theft as one in which a few wealthy artists, creators and powerful corporations are concerned about "giving away" their "product" because they are greedy and cannot change with the times to create new business models. The hundreds of thousands of people represented by the AEMI unions of the AFL–CIO are a testament to the falsity of that proposition.

Online theft and the sale of illegal CDs and DVDs are not "victimless crimes." Digital theft costs jobs and benefits. It is critical, at this important moment in the evolution of the Internet and potential Internet policy, for union members and leaders to publicly and visibly engage in a sustained effort to protect members' livelihoods, the creation and innovation that are the hallmark of their work and the economic health and viability of the creative industries in this country. The AEMI unions and other unions in U.S. entertainment stress that pirated content is devastating to the entertainment professionals who create the underlying works.

The AFL–CIO strongly supports the efforts of the AEMI unions and the Department for Professional Employees, AFL–CIO, to combat piracy. It commends their work with government and industry to develop workable solutions to protect the interests of their members. The AFL–CIO urges its affiliate unions to educate their members about the adverse impact of piracy; to support efforts to ensure that government officials and lawmakers are aware of, and support the protection of, entertainment industry jobs that will be lost to online theft; to encourage their members to respect copyright law; and to urge their members, as a matter of union solidarity, to never illegally download or stream pirated content or purchase illegal CDs and DVDs.

○